From a Grieving Mother's Heart

One Mother's Journey
Through the Loss of Her Child

By Terri Ann Leidich

Published in the United States by WriteLife
(An imprint of Boutique of Quality Books Publishing Company)
www.bqbpublishing.com

Printed in the United States of America

ISBN 978-0-9828689-1-1 (p)
ISBN 978-1-937084-01-01 (e)

Library of Congress Number: 2010910819

Cover design by Darlene Swanson • www.van-garde.com
Book design by Robin Krauss • www.lindendesign.biz

To my son Rob, for all the wonderful memories
from the twenty years we spent together.
And for the growth and wisdom
that I gained from your life . . .
and even your death.

Foreword

The loss of a child is the most devastating experience a parent can ever have. It affects us emotionally, physically, mentally, and spiritually. It feels as though someone punched their fists into our chest, tore out our heart with their bare hands, and then abandoned us to suffer alone, unsure of whether or not we will live through the ordeal.

My son was twenty years old, in college, still living at home, and a strong, positive part of my daily life. One pleasant June evening, he was visiting friends and decided to hop on a motorcycle to make a McDonald's run. Rob had driven motorcycles and had his license, but his dad and I wouldn't agree to let him purchase one. We felt much better when he was in his pickup, surrounded by strong steel.

I guess the beautiful Georgia summer night was too hard to resist. Rob put on a helmet, jumped on a motorcycle and headed to McDonald's—just a few miles away. That's the last time anyone saw him alive. A young man pulled out of an apartment complex onto a major street without looking, and my son impacted with the side of the car, breaking most major bones in his body and causing severe brain damage. He was brain dead at the scene, but his body kept functioning until 12:13 a.m. on June 8th, at which time he was pronounced dead.

On June 7th (a date that will never again be just another summer day to me), I began a horrendous journey of grief that lasted for several years. In fact, a parent never gets over the death of a child, yet the pain does ease as we learn to live around it.

Although my son died several years ago, I am often reminded that people still don't understand the journey of grief, whether they are going through it or are trying to be there for someone else who is. Many books that have been written about grief try to make sense of it or put it into a logical format, but there is no logic to the loss of a child— only gut-wrenching, debilitating pain.

At first, the loss of a child defines us and becomes who we are—a grieving parent. But over time, the experience of this terrible loss settles into being a part of the landscape of our life, instead of the sum total of it.

The journey of losing a child is a lonely one because until we travel its path, we are oblivious to the horrific agony and pain. But once we are in its grip, we feel as though we won't make it through, and we need something to assure us that we will.

When I lost my son, I wanted to know that others had walked this hellish path before me, not because I wanted someone else to feel the crippling pain, but to be assured that I wouldn't die from my grief...or to give me something to cling to so I wouldn't want to die. I wanted to be touched where it hurt—in my heart—not in my mind. I wanted to feel feelings and hear words from another parent so I would know that I wasn't alone in my agony...that others had survived the experience.

I also needed someone to meet me where I was. From those times when my mind was caught in the realms of death and dying, no longer aware of the possibilities of life, to the times when my thoughts circled so furiously that I felt as though I was losing my mind, I needed to know that others had thought similar things and felt similar feelings so I could be assured that I wasn't going crazy..

Those who surround us on a daily basis try desperately to help, yet it seems that only by walking through this "fire" can we truly know and understand the searing pain of its heat. For those with friends or family who have lost children, this book will help you understand what they are going through and why expecting them to "move on" is an unrealistic expectation. Yet you will be assured that they will eventually move forward when they have gone through their own cycle of grief.

My first years of grieving can be symbolized by a roller coaster ride with its many unexpected turns, ups, and downs. The force of the ride often cast me from mountaintops of faith into valleys of depression in the time span of a few hours. I was left breathless and confused by this terrifying voyage. But thankfully...as the years went by, the roller coaster slowly changed into a winding country road whose turns brought delightful surprises and where painful thoughts mingled with the bright, sunlit colors of wonderful memories.

My prayers go out to those of you who are traveling on the treacherous journey of grief, and my heart joins with yours in a sisterhood (or brotherhood) that we would not have chosen, but one of which we are members.

This book journals my experience through grief and demonstrates the rocky, tumultuous path that a parent travels after the death of a child. Through the pages of this book, other grieving parents can find companionship, understanding, and confirmation that the debilitating pain does eventually ease.

Chapter 1

The Agony Begins

June 7th (Day 1)

I just saw you five hours ago, Rob. You were tanned and handsome. I touched you, I hugged you, we talked. And now I'm standing in a small room in the hospital, waiting for the doctor to come in to talk with me. The nurses won't tell me where you are. They won't tell me what is happening. But I know it's bad. They wouldn't have put your Dad and me into this private room if it wasn't bad.

We were just getting ready for bed when we got the call. Dad answered it, and when he turned to look at me, his face was pale . . . he looked scared. "Rob's been in an accident," was all he needed to say. We both headed to the car and to whatever was waiting for us. We were quiet as we drove, I turned to him once and said, "He has to be okay, Chuck. He just has to."

When we got to the hospital, your friends were waiting outside by the doors to the emergency room. They said you had been in an accident. They were all talking at once, their phrases were choppy and jumbled. All I heard as I rushed by them was "accident . . . motorcycle . . . really bad."

The doctor comes in. He takes my hand and sits me down. He tells me it's bad. He tells me that you probably aren't going to make it. He tells me to pray. It's about ten-thirty at night and your accident happened at twenty-two minutes after nine.

I tell him I want to see you . . . he tells me they are still trying to save your life. So all I can do is wait.

The waiting room begins to fill as our neighbors, our friends, and your friends rush to be with us. I can barely breathe...I have just enough breath to pray for a miracle.

June 8th (Day 2) – Shortly after midnight

Now this doctor is telling me you're dead. I see him. I hear him. But I don't understand his words. He holds my hand, and Dad puts his arm around me. There are tears in their eyes. I am numb.

Dead? What does dead mean? I can't comprehend it through my blurred mind. I'm watching my body take the necessary steps and make the necessary calls. My lips form the words, and my voice carries across the wires to your grandparents, sister, aunts, and uncles: "Rob is dead. Rob has died." But what does it mean?

The doctor finally lets us see you—your body. Your face is swollen. And you're pale. When I saw you for the last time, a few hours ago, you were tan and beautiful. Where did your tan go? Does death wipe out even a tan? I place my hand on your chest. It was always so firm, but now it's not. All your major bones are broken; you feel soft.

This body on the metal table doesn't feel like you, and it doesn't really look like you. I can't see your eyes, and you're not smiling. This is not the Rob I know—the guy whose eyes are a crystal, penetrating blue, and whose smile can light up the dreariest of days. Where is Rob, the young man with a sense of humor who loves to shoot water from a squirt gun into Rica's ear to see if it will come out the other side? Rob, the man whose compassion and caring for others stretches my own? That Rob's not here. There's only a dead body lying on this steel slab. I see you. I touch you. I talk to you. But I can't stay in this room. I want to stay forever, yet I don't want to stay a moment longer. My world is crashing down around my ears.

My faith pulls strongly around me like a warm blanket. I know that your smile, your sense of humor, all that you were is either up in heaven or on its way. Are you up there,

Rob, just slightly above us? Watching us? I feel you. That's why this is all so surreal.

Many of your friends are here at the hospital; they're all crying. When will you come, Rob? Where are you? I need a hug.

Nobody told me that today was the last time I would hug you, or I would have hugged you harder. And I would have kept you with me. I wouldn't have let you be in the path of that car. I didn't know, son. I would have protected you. I would have kept you safe, and alive.

Nobody told me I'd only have you for twenty years. It's not true. I know it's not—you'll come home again. My God, my God, you've got to come home again! How can I live through this?

The doctor wants me to sit down; he wants to give me something to help me through this. You can tell they don't know me, huh, Rob? No way am I going to be drugged through this horrible ordeal. I'm going to have to feel this pain sooner or later. And I'm going to deal with it now when I'm surrounded by all this love and support. I've heard too many people talk about how lonely it gets after the funeral, after everybody goes away. No way am I going to be drugged through these first days of intense support. Besides, you know how I feel about pills. I don't take an aspirin unless the pain is about to drive me crazy, and I'm not crazy—not yet.

The pastor is here. There must be close to twenty people around us here at the hospital. Kathleen is with me. She cries as she tells me how, just weeks ago, you helped her bury her dog, the beloved pet she had for so many years. She talks of your compassion, your tears for her pain. Are you crying for me now, Rob?

I keep doing the things we have to do, and talking to the people we have to talk to; holding your friends, explaining your death. But my physical body is going crazy, as one minute I am retching over the toilet bowl, and the next minute I am holding my stomach as I brace against the cramps. One minute I am sane and logical, the next I am sobbing from the depth of my soul.

The nurse is talking to me about a phone call she has to put through. You didn't sign the donor section of your license. They want to use your body as a donor. I have to make that decision. Why did you leave that to me? I can't even think of what you might have wanted to do. I can't donate your body, your tan, beautiful body, to be cut up, pieced and donated. Will I regret it? Probably. But I keep thinking about the article in the paper the other day. A woman had donated her son's body, and now several years later, the donor recipient is dying from some disease, and they're blaming the donor. I couldn't stand that. How can I take the chance of suffering again when I can't even imagine how I'm going to make it through this?

I can accept anything but the loss of my child. Please God, please, please, please . . .

♥ ♥ ♥

Joe drove us home in the early hours of this never-ending day, and Eileen sat with me through what was left of the night. I couldn't go to bed. Each time I closed my eyes, the horrors of reality screeched through my mind. I saw your body lying on the road in a pool of blood. The doctors said you didn't suffer. They said that when you hit the side of the car, the blow to your brain caused immediate unconsciousness. For all intents and purposes, you were dead then. According to your medical records, you were "flat line" when the ambulance arrived at the hospital. But my mind, my awful, non-stop mind, keeps seeing you broken, hurting.

I get up and pace, and then I lie back down. I talk, I cry. I'm numb. This is a dream, a terrifying nightmare!

Everyone has been called and people are streaming in and out of the house. The phone doesn't stop ringing and flowers are beginning to arrive. In my head I know what is happening, but I keep hoping to see you. A small piece of my brain—the back corner—won't give up that hope.

Last night when I saw your broken, bruised body after the life had gone from it, you were still warm to my touch. Your face was puffy, bruised and cut from the impact against your helmet when you hit the car. I talked with you, I touched you. You could hear me. I know you could—I felt your presence. I felt you crying because of our pain. Is it your spirit I feel? Oh, my God, Rob, you can't be gone. You can't, you can't, you can't. We weren't through with you yet.

♥ ♥ ♥

Dad and I picked out your casket today. As I walked around that room, staring at the gaping coffins, I felt hollow. What did it matter which one we selected? Your mind, your spirit, and all we knew that was Rob is no longer here. You're in a better place; I can feel that. I can feel your spirit and its contentment, but that doesn't ease my pain. My heart and soul are racked with grief—the shell of a person in shock—suspended in time. One part of me grieves with tears and sobs; another is detached, refusing to believe, because if I really accept it and believe it, the pain will cut straight through me, slicing my heart and soul right out of my body.

Our friend Bill helped Dad and me find your final resting place today. It's next to a lake. Where else for you but near the water and in the sun? Your body can now forever lie on the beach. Well . . . it's not really a beach . . . but we'll pretend. The spot is so pretty, and there are ducks. I can see you lifting your arms in the air and running into the flock of ducks, laughing as they scatter. You were such a scoundrel, such a tease, such a delight.

How can anyone without faith go through this? I couldn't. If I believed that your broken body that will rest in this casket was all that was left of you, I would want to kill— myself or someone else. I thank God for my belief in Him. I thank Him for the way He loves me. I just don't understand why He took my son. Why mine, Lord? Why mine?

Grandma Betty is here, and Grandma Bernice and Grandpa Clyde. I want my mother and my sisters. I want to be held by them, and they are here. They give me such comfort in this time. Your sister Lori isn't going to have that. You were all she had. You were our only son; she is our only daughter. Dad and I have lost so much with your death. And we didn't have any choice. Nobody asked us. Your Dad and I have to go through this horror, and nobody asked us.

June 9th (Day 3) – Morning

I'm starting to get exhausted. I can't sleep. Every time I try, my mind races . . . thoughts, visions and fears crash through—never easing up—never letting go. My body cries out from the fatigue and the demands that have been made on it, and my mind rebels at the decisions it has been required to make.

Dad is there, ever there. But it doesn't help. It does, and then it doesn't. People keep talking about sleeping pills. I haven't agreed yet, but I'm getting so tired, and my thoughts won't leave me alone.

People are bringing me books and talking about the steps of grief...about shock, anger, depression. None of it makes sense to me.

I grasp onto things I see as merciful: the way God took you home . . . riding a motorcycle, reveling in the freedom and joy you always described. For now, I have to try to cling to that and believe that God needed you...that's why you're gone.

The horrible part of all of this is the loss—the loss of dreams and potential, the loss of your worldly love and hugs, the loss of Rob, the man. I know your spirit is here, ever present with me, but my arms long to reach out and hold you. There was something about your strong hugs that always made me feel as though I really did have a place in this world. I had given birth to you and Lori...to two beautiful people. And each day I still contributed to your life by listening to you, talking with you, encouraging you.

And now a piece of my world has been ripped away... leaving a dark, gaping, threatening hole.

Sometimes I doubt if you really knew how much you were loved. Even though I expressed it a lot, right now it doesn't seem like it was enough. For now, it feels as though

I could have said "I love you" a million times a day and it still wouldn't have adequately expressed my depth of feeling for my children, for you—my son.

June 9th (Day 3) – Late at Night

This day seems as though it's going on forever. The house is filled with people, yet I feel so alone, so empty. I am exhausted, but I cannot sleep. All the things we have gone through are just a tiny speck compared to all we have yet to endure. And I'm not sure how much farther I can make it on this hellish road.

Your girlfriend Kimmie, your best friend Rica, and I put together a photo album tonight, Rob. It's filled with your pictures—your life in photographs. You looked like a little old man shortly after you were born; somehow there was already wisdom in your eyes. I never noticed that until after you were dead. As you grew through the years, you always had a smile on your face, and through all the different haircuts, your white blonde hair always refused to do anything but lay softly against your head. As I followed your life in the picture album, I saw a young boy grow into a man, and I saw all the things we did as a family. I had taken so many of these things for granted, but now they are precious memories.

Remember my favorite picture from your childhood? You were about three years old, and it was Christmas morning. You were dressed only in your t-shirt and training pants. You had a toy gunbelt strapped around your waist, a cowboy hat on your head, and a red bandanna around your mouth. I loved that picture! You hated it. You'd always say, "Oh, Mom, not that one!" whenever I would dig it out.

I'm very proud of the pictures of you and Kim when you went to your first prom at your high school last year, then her prom one month ago. You looked so handsome and grown up. I will treasure those pictures and the video we took, for as long as I live.

Why didn't I take more pictures this last year? Why didn't somebody tell me this would be my last chance?

June 10th (Day 4)

My heart has been ripped from my breast. Life has stopped making sense. I'm numb. I'm a zombie…a walking, talking, empty shell.

My mind is an evil thing that fills me with pain and regrets, but I'll fight it. I will fight my way from this black hole of endless pain into sunshine—somewhere, somehow—where I can remember the good and happy special times.

Your visitation was tonight. We had a closed casket. I didn't like the way you looked and you would have hated people seeing you for the last time like that. Your face was still puffy from your injuries, and your lips were painted pink. Kimmie said you would have hated the pink lips. I'm sure you did.

It was strange kneeling before your coffin, touching you, running my hand through your hair the way I used to do. This time you couldn't yell at me not to mess your hair.

Do you remember a few weeks go when I stayed home from work because I was sick? You stretched out at the foot of the bed and talked with me. I can still see your face as it rested on your hands. Your eyes danced as you talked about your dreams and grew serious as you shared your concerns. I ran my fingers through your hair. "Just always do the best you can, Rob. Look at your options and make your choices." I had no idea the limited amount of time you had for making those choices.

I used to have such a fear about death and dead people. Not about dying, but what it was like to touch someone who had died, or to be in a funeral home or a graveyard. That aversion has disappeared now that you are dead. It was so natural to touch you. (Months later I will regret I didn't hold you.)

In amongst my grief was my natural curiosity. You had staples in your head, Rob. They were skillfully covered by your hair, but I saw them, I felt them. Did they cut your head open at the hospital to relieve the pressure? Did they do the best they could? How do I know if they were good doctors? I don't. I can only have faith that they were.

Or did they cut your head for the embalming? What is embalming? What do they do? These thoughts tumbled through my mind as I knelt in front of you. Was I going crazy? I didn't know at that moment, and several hours later, I still don't know. I think I am, but I'm not certain.

As I knelt by you, I talked to you. I touched you. I told you funny remembrances of your childhood. We were there tonight together, you and I. Then I knew I had to get up and let Lori and Dad have quiet time with you. That's when the hard part hit. That's when I knew I was seeing you for the last time. That's when I knew I had to walk away and leave my son alone . . . lying in his coffin. Never would I touch you again . . . never would I run my fingers through your wonderful blonde hair...never again could I place a kiss on your sweet cheek. Panic seized me and I felt as though I could never get up from that spot before your coffin. I understand now how hysteria can set in.

Thankfully, my strength and faith, somewhere from the very depths, surfaced—its voice was tiny but there—and I prayed: "Dear God, give me the strength to be able to leave the side of my son. To face all the people who will come to show us they care and to face the long, empty road before me." As He always does, my Father in heaven gave me strength. I breathed deeply, kissed your cheek one last time, touched my fingers to your lips, stood up and left the room. When I returned after Lori and Dad had been with you, your casket was closed.

♥ ♥ ♥

The funeral home was filled with people and flowers. Could you see all the flowers, Rob? They were everywhere. The people at the funeral home started placing them all around the room, but I didn't want that. I wanted the flowers around your casket. I wanted people to know how much you were loved by simply seeing all those flowers surrounding— almost embracing—your coffin.

I was impressed by the number of friends you had...the many lives you had impacted. And you were only twenty-and-a-half-years-old. Can you imagine the impact you could have had if you had lived for ninety years? Why weren't you given that chance?

We brought the photo album with us to the funeral home, and I'm glad we did. Instead of looking at your dead, bruised body, your friends and ours were able to see—through pictures—the smile that was so often on your face and the twinkle that was almost always in your eyes. In several photographs, you were giving me hugs—for birthday gifts, or Christmas—and I treasure those pictures. They will always remind me of the many hugs and mutual love we shared.

I walked, I talked, I did what I had to do. Your friends broke my heart. Their faces showed the shock of coming face-to-face with mortality. They all thought they were invincible—just as you did. They don't know what to do with the proof that they're not.

Alan asked if the coffin could be opened long enough for your friends to place the baseball, basketball and nerf ball in it. And your shorts—those ragged old jean shorts that you loved. If you'd had a say, you probably would have preferred to be buried in them. But, a mother has to say 'no' occasionally.

Your friends all signed the balls and the shorts, so you could take a part of them with you. I hurt for them . . . I hurt for me . . . I hurt for Dad and Lori. Life hurts so damn bad right now . . . I could scream from the agony.

I asked Holly, our Associate Pastor, to close the visitation with a prayer and a reading of the Twenty-third Psalm. She started reading the verse, and her voice choked with tears. She couldn't go on. My heart reached out to her and loved her for caring. I got up from the chair where I was sitting, walked over, put my arm around her and began to read the Psalm. My mother says I'm very strong. I don't think so. I think I'm walking in a fog. I'm acting and reacting, but if I stopped to feel, I would die.

June 10th (Day 4)

My heart has been ripped from my breast. Life has stopped making sense. I'm numb. I'm a zombie…a walking, talking, empty shell.

My mind is an evil thing that fills me with pain and regrets, but I'll fight it. I will fight my way from this black hole of endless pain into sunshine—somewhere, somehow— where I can remember the good and happy special times.

Your visitation was tonight. We had a closed casket. I didn't like the way you looked and you would have hated people seeing you for the last time like that. Your face was still puffy from your injuries, and your lips were painted pink. Kimmie said you would have hated the pink lips. I'm sure you did.

It was strange kneeling before your coffin, touching you, running my hand through your hair the way I used to do. This time you couldn't yell at me not to mess your hair.

Do you remember a few weeks go when I stayed home from work because I was sick? You stretched out at the foot of the bed and talked with me. I can still see your face as it rested on your hands. Your eyes danced as you talked about your dreams and grew serious as you shared your concerns. I ran my fingers through your hair. "Just always do the best you can, Rob. Look at your options and make your choices." I had no idea the limited amount of time you had for making those choices.

I used to have such a fear about death and dead people.

June 11th (Day 5)

We laid your body to rest today, son. Were you there? I think so. Did you see the mass of flowers flanking your coffin in the church? Did you hear the music and see your friends all somber as they ushered your casket in and out? Did you hear the beautiful sermon that Holly gave; the words to the song that I had written a month ago; the special poem we read at your grave? Did you hear the ducks as they joined in the singing at your graveside? You were probably egging them on!

Did you see the long line of cars that followed us to the grave today? Or the oncoming cars that pulled to the side of the road as a sign of respect? It is such a thoughtful and beautiful gesture. Dad and I were touched and humbled, but what a hellish way to discover it.

I did the hardest thing today that I have ever done in my life. I walked away from your grave, leaving you there, for...forever. What a long, long time forever is . . .

I know you loaned him to me, Lord
my tiny son so sweet.
To feed, to clothe, to guide, to love
until you called him home above.
But Lord so soon?
I question you.
I had him but a while . . .
this son so precious and so dear,
my own sweet youngest child.
I was prepared to say goodbye
as he went out the door.
But I really wasn't ready, Lord
that it be forevermore.

June 14th (Day 8)

I wore one of your shirts today, Rob. It was my way of wrapping your arms around me. I kept remembering the last time I saw you alive. You were sitting on the sofa in the living room. We talked for a while, then I went in to get dressed so Dad and I could go to Kim's graduation. You and Kim had had an argument and you weren't sure if you were going to go to her graduation. When I came out, you were gone. I never saw you alive again. Why didn't I insist that you go with us?

The world just keeps going on. How can it? You're gone! How can people smile, laugh, work, love? But they do. I can't...and people expect me to. Already they are telling me you would want me to get on with my life. I want to tell them to get a life of their own and let me deal with mine!

How do I tell people who care about me to get out of my face? You'd probably be able to tell me how. When my insight didn't work, yours did. What a loss I have suffered!

What's life all about? We live, we die, and life goes on. What was your life for? Your death has impacted a lot of people, but will the impact last in anyone's life but mine?

I feel like a big, bloppy mass with no form or purpose. I don't feel close to anyone right now. It's as if no one has lived up to my dreams or expectations except you. Or is it just the halo that death places around our memory which pales our humanness?

June 16th (Day 10)

I can't grip the reality of you being dead. I look at Kim's prom picture, taken just a month ago, and I see a vibrant, handsome young man. Then I think about the body in the coffin—a body that was so beaten up it didn't even resemble you.

Nothing in my mind connects me to the reality of your death.

June 17th (Day 11)

I feel hopeless today, Rob. A majority of my life has been put into you and Lori—carrying you, having you, loving you, planning for, dreaming with, and guiding you. Now it feels as though it's all gone . . . all that you were is no longer available for me to see, touch, hold. A part of my life has been whisked away and all I'm left with are the memories and the pain.

Always the pain . . . some bitter: at the man who carelessly took your life; at the biological father who has never been there for you in your life, yet dares to claim you as a son in your death. Pain for the regrets of the things I now wish I'd done. Yet, at the same time, sweet pain from the memories of time spent together: your hug and phone calls on the day you died; the day a few weeks ago when you curled up on my bed and talked the wonderful agonies and joys of youth; memories of the day you graduated from high school and how proud Dad and I were; sweet memories of the day we signed up for college classes together, and how proudly we introduced each other as mother and son.

What do we do with the smashed hopes and dreams? What do we do with this gut-wrenching ache twisting deep inside of us?

I cling desperately to my faith, trying to hold steadfast to a tiny trickle of light from eternity . . . trying to hope and continue to believe in something greater.

June 18th (Day 12)

You've been dead a little over a week, yet when I talk about you, some people stare over my shoulder into space; some try to change the subject; and others look so uncomfortable that, out of guilt, I change the subject. It was okay to talk about you through the funeral, and now it's not? Do they think that I can shut off the feelings, the pain of loss, the intense, gut-wrenching sorrow because you're now buried? I gave twenty years of my life to you, my child, and you were suddenly killed—snapped away from me! I need to experience my emotions, pain, sorrow, grief, anger, soft memories, pride, faith and trust in a gracious God.

Sometimes my mind plays tricks with me and shuts the door on my memory of the living Rob, only letting me feel the presence of the Rob I've had to adjust to since your death. This scares me. I feel that you are so indelibly imprinted on my heart, mind, and soul that I can see every feature of your body. Then the next minute, a fuse in my mind blows, and everything is blurry as I fight to remember the last time I saw you.

I cannot heal in a week. Perhaps it will take me years, or even a lifetime, of needing to talk about you, my pride and joy, and a wonderful part of my life. I need someone, or many someones, who will let me do that.

My dreams of you awaken me as the agony of reality rips me into emotional pieces. Just a moment ago in my dreams, you were alive and bounding through the door with, "I'm home! Where is everybody?" Your presence in the corners of my mind is so strong that awakening is as painful as being shredded into thin, bloody strips. I don't want to wake up. I want the dream to be real. Life is too hideous, too cruel, too empty to face. For right now, I'll take my dreams.

June 19th (Day 13)

I feel so angry tonight I could knock my fist through someone's face. It appears that the young man who carelessly pulled out in front of you—and killed you—has no insurance. If he wasn't drinking, which is yet to be determined by the blood tests, he'll most likely be charged with a misdemeanor, which will probably mean a fine of about $300 and a slap on the hand. If he was drinking, he'll be charged with a felony, and there is no way to even guess the consequences.

But he has no insurance and no assets to help us with the financial havoc he has caused. Savings are for college planning. But death? Does this young man have any idea what it costs to bury the man he killed? I want to beat my fists against him and scream at him. I want him punished. He killed my son, dammit! He's got to pay for that! My anger is so strong that I'd easily invoke the biblical "eye for an eye" rule if I could. Yet that's the most exasperating part—there's not much I can do. It's out of my hands.

June 20th (Day 14)

Some days it would be easier not to write about my feelings, and this is one of those days. One moment I expect you to come bouncing in the door, and the next awful moment I realize you never will again. The pain of grief knocks me across the face one minute, and my faith lifts me the next.

I spent a long time talking with Chris and Rica about you today. While doing so, I felt exhilarated that you live so strongly in their memories. Not long afterward, I was sitting on the kitchen floor sobbing because we wouldn't be making more memories.

June 21st (Day 15)

I ate a bunch of chocolate today. I just stuffed it into my mouth and now my head and muscles ache, and my stomach is upset.

I need people around me, but I want to be alone. I need the busyness of work and activities, but I don't want to get out of bed. I hate the world and everything in it that is active and alive, yet I treasure life.

I fluctuate between feeling as though God is picking on me and basking in His grace and love. I don't have a lot of tolerance for my ambivalence toward God, so I sure hope He has more patience with me than I do.

I believe God called you home, yet I hate the man who caused your death. How can I hate him if he's an instrument of God? All of life makes no sense to me now, yet it is dearer than it has ever been.

I'm scared of losing everyone since the reality of death and our fragility has hit me in the heart. Our human vessels seem as delicate as egg shells, capable of being crushed by a single firm squeeze from life.

Writing calms me. Why don't I write instead of eat? Why didn't someone else die instead of you?

I don't know.

How can words ever convey my deep sorrow or the cavernous hole this loss has left in my life? It is a pain beyond comprehension.

June 24th (Day 18)

I went back to work today and it kept me busy, but nothing can take away the pain. Unexpected memories burst into my mind and sent shock waves of agony through me, emotionally knocking me to the ground.

Today when Danielle was away from her desk, I answered the phone. It was Janice's son asking for her. Just a simple, ordinary happening on a typical day, but it drove a knife into my gut as I realized that I will never again get a call from you. Rob, Rob, Rob, how can I make it through life without you? You were such a part of me. You were flesh of my flesh. You were my dreams and my hopes, my expectations of life. You gave me proof that my optimistic approach to life would pay off. Now my optimism is lying shattered against the ragged rocks of life as evil laughter echoes through my ears.

When I get tired, it is worse . . . I feel hopeless and don't really see any reason to put effort into anything. I know there's a reason and I know I'll get through this, but God help me . . . I want to scream: "I WANT MY SON BACK!" I would give anything to hug you again, scold you again, help you with your Algebra and English again.

I feel as though life is picking on me. I just get adjusted to one difficulty and I get slapped with another. Still, I won't give up. I won't. There is a fire deep inside of me that struggles to burn, no matter how many times it is doused with water. But this last one has been a torrential rain that is trying to wash out even the dying embers of hope.

Why do I want to recover from this when I'll just be hit with something else? I'm terrified with the thought that life is just a series of losses, and mine have just begun. Why the hell do I want to recover to just get ready for more pain? It doesn't make any sense.

Is God just a non-feeling entity that sits up there playing chess with our lives . . . mercilessly knocking the pieces off the board at will?

He has completely toppled my game board, and does He care? My mind wants to shout . . . "No! No! No!" Yet, deep inside, I know none of that is true.

Moment by moment
Dear Lord I pray,
Give me the strength
To face each day.
Weakened and grieving
Sunk in despair,
I desperately need to
Feel that you care.

June 26th (Day 20)

In the mornings it doesn't hurt quite so badly, son. Yet when I'm not torn apart with pain, I get scared that I'm forgetting you already, and I hate that thought. I refuse to ever forget you. What is life all about if we die and we're forgotten?

At night when I'm tired, the pain and loneliness once again sear my heart, and I feel as though this suffering will never lessen.

This grief for me is a roller coaster ride of emotions and thoughts. I miss you so much, but I'm so proud of the young man you were. As Robin commented to me yesterday: "Look what you raised." You were a beautiful young man with a wonderful head on your shoulders. We were so blessed to have you! Why can't I just take comfort in that and quit hurting so badly? I don't know. It's one of the many unanswered questions I have.

June 27th (Day 21)

We went to your grave today, Rob, and brought you flowers, but I know you're not there. I can feel you with me every day, so sitting at your grave seems futile.

We got a check from the college today. They refunded your last quarter fees. I cried. The unexpected things like that make it harder, yet make it easier.

I could so easily close up . . . shutting off any warmth or feeling. I try to have an interest in life, but I'm not sure I want to.

Tonight, Kim, Chris, and Rica brought over a movie, and we watched it while we ate crazy bread and pizza. I thought of you a lot . . . of all the crazy movies you used to bring home, and the many pizzas we shared—all the memories!

I remember Stone Mountain on the Fourth of July in the rain with your broken umbrella. You looked so funny. And Chuckie Cheese on Kim's birthday when we played the games together. Or when we all went to the movies—you and Kim, Dad and I—and you picked the movie, which was awful!

I remember the times you and I went to the movies or dinner by ourselves. Remember when that lady called me a cradle robber? She thought we were on a date instead of mother and son. You said it was because I didn't look old enough to be your mother. Such a charmer!

Remember the time we went to the Thai restaurant, and you loved it? You took your friends back, and they all thought it was gross. You always were wonderfully adventurous.

My memories could fill pages! Remember when you were about eight years old and Lori was about ten? She was apparently really getting on your nerves because you rigged a cup of water underneath the canopy on her bed and when she sat down, the water poured right on her head.

She was furious! I was impressed with your ingenuity! And apparently I didn't hold back my laughter very well because Lori is still a bit indignant when she tells the story.

You brought so much laughter into our lives and apparently into your friends' lives as well. I've heard so many funny stories about you that I might not have known for many years . . . they were rather mischievous stories. Like the bubbles in the hot tub at our house in Dallas. You said you didn't know how they got there. We know now . . . about the bottle of shampoo you kids poured in and the mountain of billowy shampoo clouds that erupted from the spa. As your friend Marc told the story, I could see all of you as you formed hats and ears and beards out of the suds. I thought it was hilarious. I don't know if Dad shared my glee. He was the one who cleaned the tub and filter in the aftermath!

And now we also know about the time that you and Marc got Dad's truck stuck in the mud right up to the floorboards. You had promised to pick him up at the airport, so he gave you the keys to his four-wheel-drive pickup. Guess the temptation was too great. You and Marc apparently took it off-road to do some four-wheeling and got really stuck. You had to have someone with a winch pull you out and then you apparently used up a lot of quarters in the car wash as you had to clean the mud off—from both the outside and the inside! Marc said you were both scared to death that Dad would ring your necks, but I guess your cleanup job was pretty good because he never suspected. He actually smiled a bit when Marc told the story.

That's what I miss, most Rob: the laughter that surrounded you. Sure, you had a serious side, but mischief always lurked just below the surface!

After the movie tonight, I started sobbing. The pain was so deep I wrapped my arms around my stomach as if I could stop it or make it go away. I wanted you back. Your friends are wonderful and I love them, but I want you!

June 28th (Day 22)

I had a bad day today. Dad and I had a spat this morning; I started crying and couldn't stop. Then the demands of everyone at work crowded in. I feel as though I am in a box that has been catapulted to the bottom of the sea. As long as I keep the box closed up tight, I can breathe. But, I'm running out of oxygen, and when I try to peek my head out to get some life-giving air, the salt water of grief, mixed with life, pours in and drowns me.

June 29th (Day 23)

My goals have changed. Now that you're gone and Lori is so far away, everything I've been working for in my life is gone. You were the one I still had at home to help through college, to love, to guide. My demanding job was important as an example to you of what life requires and how to meet those challenges, yet still take care of yourself. My college was important, my writing was important. Now, I don't know what's important. I feel like a boat adrift in a sea that has no life, no waves to challenge me, only those that devour me. And the fight that used to be in me is gone. Now I could just sit still and let the waves wash over me until I drown.

Feelings whirl
and twirl in
a hollow heart.
Empty, alone,
confused.
Searching, pulling,
seeking a greater being,
a higher power,
an answer.

July 3rd (Day 27)

I must be in a new stage because I wish people would leave me alone. I'm tired and emotionally stretched to my limit. Sometimes I miss you so badly the pain burns inside of me, and last night was one of them. I didn't want to deal with it. I rented some movies and wanted to just lose myself, and I got all kinds of phone calls.

Now this morning, I feel triple-exhausted. I just need space. I need people to back off. But they don't know that . . . and how do I tell them? When someone is calling long-distance, how do I tell them I just don't want to talk to anybody? Maybe they could ask. That would help a lot.

July 4th (Day 28)

The Fourth of July was hard for me today. It's filled with memories. Holidays give me dates of memories to hang on to or to be tortured by. The rest of the days blend into just living, but on holidays, we always concentrated on family, and those are the memories that are so bittersweet.

I felt broken today. I watched your prom and graduation videos and yelled at Dad and accused him of recording over the Christmas video.

I gave him such an awful time. To me it looks like, after just four weeks, he's completely over his grief, and I hate him for that. A human life is worth four weeks of sorrow, and that's it? My sorrow feels as though it will never leave. I feel as though it is so indelibly engraved in me that I will never be without it.

Rob, why did you have to leave me?

When you first died, I felt as though I could feel your spirit, but I don't feel that as much lately. Once in a while I do, but it's not always comforting, and I don't know if that's me or you.

Gentle angel up above
looking down at me
with love.
Cradle me with
loving care
assuring me
you're really there.
Let me feel
your gentle smile
and stay with me
for just a while,
While I adjust to you
up there.
My special angel
in heavenly air.

July 8th (Day 32)

I have never before encountered anything in my life that has so knocked the wind out of me. In retrospect, everything else looks like it was easy: my parents' alcoholism, the abuse, the divorce, the co-dependency. It all felt like a cakewalk compared to this!

One of the hardest things I've had to deal with in all this, is the mortality of mankind. Somehow in life we walk around thinking that it's only the other guy who is susceptible to all the dangers that lurk in our world. Now it would be so easy to become paranoid. There are so many things out there that could hurt us or kill us. It would be easy to hide away from life right now.

It was a month ago yesterday that you had your accident. And a month ago this morning that you died. I'm doing better than I was, but the littlest thing will set me off.

Last night we went to a "Picnic in the Park with the Atlanta Symphony" with Kathy and Bill. I was doing fairly well yesterday, then an ambulance came to the concert because somebody was sick. And my mind took it from there. I imagined your broken, bleeding body being picked up off the street and put into an ambulance while the EMTs frantically worked to save your life during the rush to the hospital. The whole scene played over and over in my mind, and I began to cry. Dad didn't comfort me, which made me cry more.

♥ ♥ ♥

Now I'm positive that heaven has layers. It never seemed fair to me that I could spend my whole life being good so I could go to heaven, and somebody else could live life being a thief or murderer and then just before dying they ask God for forgiveness, and boom, they're in heaven too. Now

I realize that they may end up in heaven as a janitor, and you with your beautiful pure heart will end up an engineer. Yet, I chuckle when I think that. Down here, you struggled with your own faith and belief. You fought against accepting my ideas of what God and eternal life were all about, yet you believed, sometimes stronger than I did, in a Greater Being, and you had much more awe about the beauty of life than I. In that way, you took after Dad and learned from him.

The subject of faith and belief in something greater is so complex. I hate it that we as humans, especially Christians, seem to have the compulsion or need to put everyone else's faith into a little box that matches our own. I guess we keep trying to give our own some credence.

You taught me so much…about living life to the fullest and about caring for people. I really need to pull that lesson close to my heart right now because I don't care much about anyone or anything but you. I'm not caring for myself or taking care of myself, and with God's help, I'll try to do that.

July 13th (Day 37)

We found out last night that the man who killed you does have insurance. That took a big load off of Dad. Our grief has been hard enough to handle, but having to deal with financial stuff and using money that was intended for your education for a funeral instead has been overwhelming. And Dad's been handling all of that . . . I can barely function let alone think about money. I just keep clinging to the fact that God has never let me down, and I know he won't stop now. He doesn't keep me out of the fires of life, but He always walks through the flames with me.

We had a barbecue last night, son. Your Aunt Kathy and Uncle Rich are here for the weekend, so we invited the neighbors over. I really enjoy the kids you hung out with. I enjoyed them when you were alive, but in the face of all we lost, they've become dearer still. We've started a Sunday afternoon movie tradition. We began by taking Kimmie and Chris to see Robin Hood—Rica joined us for the next one, and Alan is going to join us next Sunday.

The last five weeks have been the most difficult ones I've ever been through, but I've made it. I feel much more hyper and nervous than I used to. Inside, I often feel shaky. It's got to be from all that my emotional system has been through. And lately, I'm back on the sugary foods. I've got to stop them. I'm killing my body and I can feel you nagging at me. You were always so big on taking care of our bodies and our health.

July 14th (Day 38)

It's seven o'clock in the morning, and I'm sitting on the patio. I can hear the birds singing; it's so beautiful out here. The traffic is starting to get heavier, and it's messing with my serenity, so I guess it's time to get on with my day.

Your Aunt Kathy and I are going to bring more fresh flowers to your grave, and we'll bring some bread to feed the ducks. Dad goes to your grave more often than I do. I think of you every day, but going to your grave is hard. It brings into my mind the reality of your body lying beneath the ground. I can't handle that very often right now.

It was hard for your Aunt Kathy to stand at your grave today. She didn't say a lot, yet her face registered many levels of pain. Kathy lost a husband many years ago, and as she stood at your grave, I believe she felt not only remnants of her pain those many years ago, but also her pain around your death and my grief.

People close to me seem to try to hide their pain to protect me. Don't they know that it won't hurt as bad as staying apart from me does? It's in the sharing that we help each other.

July 16th (Day 40)

The young man who killed you has minimum insurance, Rob. That makes me angrier than when he had no insurance at all. I'm not sure why. I think it's because your life has now been reduced to numbers and dollar signs.

Dad and I went to your grave on Sunday. We stopped and bought some fresh flowers like we do every week. When we got there, your vase was full. Kimmie, Rica, Chris, and Alan had been there ahead of us. The vase was filled with bright carnations and daisies, petunias formed a circle around the base of the vase, and a rose lay on the ground where "Brother" had been scratched into the dirt. I cried, Rob. Seeing how much you were and are loved makes me feel good and sad at the same time.

♥ ♥ ♥

The days get easier as we settle into a routine. I still have a huge hole inside of me, but the edges aren't as raw. I don't know, maybe I'm still in shock, maybe reality hasn't set in yet.

The toxicology tests came back from the State; both you and the other guy were clear. I don't know if that means he wasn't drinking at all, or if he was just under the legally drunk number. He has been charged with Second Degree Manslaughter. I want to be there when he goes to court. I want to see this man...the man, who after taking your life, let us live with our grief and the financial impact for a month without contacting us or his insurance company. Is he just young and unaware of responsibilities, or is he uncaring, with no value for human life? I don't know if I hate him because he killed you and I have to live with the pain caused by his mistake, or if I have compassion for him because he has to live with it too. I won't know until I see him . . . see his eyes. If his eyes are cold and lifeless, I will hate him for what he's done and for what he's caused in our lives. But if his eyes are filled with the pain of what his actions have done to both his life and ours, I can have compassion for him. At least, I think I can. Yet, he's taken one of the dearest things in life away from me.

July 18th (Day 42)

I feel I need to write, yet I don't want to. The conflict of your death rages within me, and I feel that my writing could be deeper and more compassionate because of the loss I suffer. Yet when I try to write and the words come out, they fall futilely onto the paper the way seeds scatter on hard, unfertile ground. I want to make sense out of your death and out of life itself with my words, but I can't seem to do that. I want to write strong, compelling thoughts that will eventually help others so that my loss won't have been in vain. I want to create something in your memory so you will never be forgotten, but I fall so short of the task.

Deep inside of me
resides a soul.
An empty, hollow soul.
A shell of what I could be,
unseeing of what I am.
A turning, churning soul
swallowed by aloneness
and fear.
A grasping, clinging,
unyielding soul,
waiting to be heard,
filled with pain,
faith and belief.

July 20th (Day 44)

My energy level is still low, Rob, and my mind is often on you, but I don't feel the deep sadness right now. I've met people who are still in the throws of depression after six months or a year or two. Why am I doing so well? Is this lack of sadness just another stage I'm going through . . . one that won't last?

Silent angel, hovering over me,
gently placing kisses on my cheeks.

You are such a part of my life now,
how can I .grieve that you are gone?

I don't have you in physical form,
I can't feel the strength of your hugs,

But I still feel the gentleness
of your caring and I hear the ring of your laughter.

I no longer hear your voice with my ears,
I hear it through my heart and soul.

Silent angel hovering over me,
you continue to touch my life.

We've changed roles, you and I.
I was the one who guided you,

Now you lead me by the hand,
softly whispering through my mind
thoughts and ideas
that are more like you than me.

July 25th (Day 49)

I was looking at Dad's and my passport this morning, son, and I wish we had taken you to Cancun with us. We said we'd do it next year and you said you had plenty of years—but you didn't

The days are heavy on my soul. I no longer know who I am or what life is for me. Someone has turned my life upside down, the pieces are scattered everywhere, and many are smashed to smithereens. I have just enough energy to put my life on its side, let alone put it upright and try to pick up the scattered contents. Even when I have the energy to do that, what about the broken parts? They can't be replaced. What you brought into my life can't be duplicated. What you were to me cannot be substituted. Therefore, my life is no longer the same, nor am I.

July 27th (Day 51)

I called a counselor yesterday. I have an appointment next Wednesday. I am so different from who I was that it frightens me. I took pride in knowing myself and in being emotionally healthy. Now, neither of those things is true. I don't know where to start, or even if I should start right now. All I know is that I need some help so I don't go backward.

I miss you. Not one particular thing, but all you were, all that your life was about. I can't feel you as much lately, and I miss that closeness. If I can't have you in person, I need your spirit close to me. I've lost one of the most precious things in my life. Why? I can't find an answer. Do you know the reasons, Rob? Looking down from God's perspective, does life make sense? Does my life make sense? Does it have a purpose? Can you help me understand and fulfill that purpose?

I feel I'm supposed to write, but my writing seems so simple and imperfect. How can it have a purpose? Yet, in your short, imperfect life, you had a great purpose. You touched a lot of lives.

God, please hold my son,
since I can't.

Assure him that he's special,
since I can't.

Give him all he needs to grow
and guide him on his way,
since I can't.

And when he does something wonderful,
let him know it,
since I can't.

Enjoy him, Lord,
every special thing about him,
since I can't.

And hold him safe in heaven's arms,
until I get there,
so I can.

July 29th (Day 53)

Am I just coming out of the shock of this whole bizarre thing? Perhaps I am. I don't know. I just know that I hurt more now than ever and not just an emotional hurt, but physical pain as well. I have a headache I can't shake. I constantly have a sore throat, and my muscles hurt like they've been put in a vice. I've never thought about the physical pain of grief before or how horribly all-consuming and painful grief is.

And I'm changed. I'm angry and not so nice. I'm not angry about anything in particular, I'm just angry about and at everything. Lives around me seem to keep going on as usual while a part of my life has been torn from my arms. Why?

He was one of my reasons for living;
the brightest of all twinkling stars.
I clung to all he was
the way moisture sits
gently on a morning leaf.

My heart cries out and rebels
at his never living again.
Unfairness ignites my anger
like a match ignites a
pile of dried pine needles.

Hopelessness envelopes my spirit
and carries it to the
bitter depths of hell
leaving only a broken, empty shell.

I cannot think of tomorrow
when all my yesterdays
have been gathered together
and smashed like a helpless ship
by angry ocean waves
against razor-edged rocks.

July 30th (Day 54)

My sister Kathy says I'm dealing not only with grief, but with "empty nest syndrome." I'm not sure I'm going to make it through this one, son. I'm not sure I want to and that's scary. I'm not suicidal or anything like that, I just feel like curling into a ball and never getting up.

Your sister called tonight. She said she had a feeling I needed her, and I did. I just cried and cried. You'd think I'd be all cried out by now.

I think I'm still in the denial stage. A part of me refuses to accept the reality of never seeing you again in this life. How can that be? How can I have birthed you, nurtured you, raised you, protected you, gotten you through the teenage years and the years of trouble and woe you had, to lose you when you were on such a splendid path? How does that make any sense? What was that all about if I was fated to lose you anyway?

Denial? Hell yes, I'm in denial! How can I possibly look this ugly monster called grief in the face when I'm convinced it will devour me?

Oh grief,
you many tentacled monster
standing in the middle of my world,
pulling me toward
the open pit of darkness.

Confusing me with your many arms
of anger, sorrow, guilt and pain.
Ever, ever pulling me toward the darkness
as if no light will ever shine
in my world again.

Hideous monster,
how did I not know the forcefulness
of your existence
until you wrapped your vicious arms
around me and squeezed my life
from my very soul?

August 2nd (Day 57)

Pain evens out in life, doesn't it? Isn't that what life is about? Please, *please*, somebody tell me what life is all about.

At this very minute in my life, it seems as if God takes all that is good. Why did I work so hard to guide you into a good life, only to lose you? Had I known, would I have changed anything? Probably not!

I treasure the twenty-and-a-half years of memories. But why couldn't they have been sixty years of memories? Only God has that answer, and He's not telling me!

Doubt...
oh dark, circling emotion,
pulling me down, down
drowning me in fear and pain.

Doubt...
dark, hopeless feeling,
painful, aching feeling,
circling, circling around me.

Pulling...
pulling me down
into your dreary depths.

August 8th (Day 63)

Ed died this week, Rob. Exactly two months from the day you died. And he was on a motorcycle too. He had been drinking, and it was raining. He hydroplaned, lost control of the bike, his body was thrown forty feet into a telephone pole, and the rest is history.

Why am I telling you? You know. You and Ed have probably already had a reunion of souls. Help me understand. Ed was drinking and driving. Why? Son, please help me understand how we are failing you guys. Why is drinking so often the main recreational activity of so many young people?

Life after life is being lost. Why? I keep asking God the same question. Somehow if I could just help one young person...but I feel so helpless. I'm here, I hold out my arms, open our home; but how can I get into their heads?

It's been two months, and I'm facing the fact that I have to eventually let go of you. Your departure has left an empty black hole in my life, and I miss you every minute of my day. The pain isn't as sharp right now, yet it's deeper as the reality of forever in this life seeps into my brain.

September 15th (Day 101)

I haven't written for awhile because it's been such a roller coaster month for me. I thought if I got away from thinking about your death, I would be able to keep myself on a more even emotional keel. And it worked—some.

The hardest part of this past month has been the loneliness. I miss you so badly—your hugs, your smile, your sense of humor—all that you were and all that you were growing to be. I miss your dreams, your plans, your schemes.

People wound me badly by not asking about me or talking about you. They seem to think that silence is better than saying the wrong thing. I don't agree. How do I know they care about me or cared about you unless they say so? Even if they said "I want to talk about Rob, but I'm so afraid that it will hurt you, or that I'll say the wrong thing." That would be better for me than silence.

I want to talk about you all the time. It helps me deal with your being gone. Yesterday's memories are all I have of you. I don't get to have any tomorrows. I'm accepting that, and I'm so very glad that I have the memories, but I need to bring them out very frequently and enjoy their warmth so I can deal with the finality of your death.

You know me, I have always been the eternal optimist. Now I'm struggling to keep that up. I've always believed that in every situation there is good. So I've tried hard to find good things, even now. One good thing keeps emerging in the blur of negatives—you'll be forever young and we'll always remember you at the peak of your life, because that's when you died.

The last day you were alive is so cemented in my mind. You were happy with your life that afternoon. I remember the hugs and kidding about your grades. I told you that you had to maintain Bs if you wanted me to continue to pay for your classes. You grinned and said you had an A in Algebra and C in Business Communications. Then with another grin you put your arm around me. "That's a B average, Mom. Does that count?"

That last day with you was so beautiful! Yet, there were so many beautiful days in our lives together. Now the hard part is that Dad and I have to go on without you. We're learning, but it's a slow and often painful process.

I have no one to mother. You were my last child, my baby. With your death, our house became tomb-like. All its vitality seemed to be drained out when you were laid to rest. And that vitality will never be back. True, the house is taking on a new form of life as Dad and I adjust to our aloneness, but it's not the same, and never will be.

Was there a meaning and reason for your death? Did God take you to teach somebody a lesson, to help somebody's life? I don't know. Everybody has different thoughts and beliefs on that. Some people don't believe God had anything to do with your death. I do. I had to find the answer that works for me. I believe God took you home because He has a purpose for you in heaven. To God, death is not bad because He can see the whole picture. He knows what eternal life is like. He doesn't have to try to fill in the blanks the way we do.

I'll never forget when, shortly after your death, I was beseeching God, "Why? Why Rob? Why my son who was good and had so much potential?" And in my mind, my answer came so clearly: "Because I'm building a foundation, and you don't do that with scrap metal."

Gentle angel sleeping nigh,
can you hear my painful sigh,
of loneliness and dreams forsaken,
a future of hope badly shaken,
by the empty cavern in my heart,
where you were once a living part?

September 27th (Day 113)

Well Rob, today I celebrated my birthday. It was my first birthday in twenty years without you, but it was a good day. So many good and wonderful people reached out to me. I got so many flowers, my office started looking like a florist shop. It was great!

But I sure would like one of your super hugs for my birthday. It's sad to think I'll never get one again. My thoughts of the future still aren't clear, but they're getting a little bit better. I'm so sorry I have to live the rest of my years without you, but I realize I'm fortunate to continue to receive the gift of life. You, my precious son, were also a gift, one that unfortunately, I got to keep for such a little while.

A lot of your friends remembered me, and Kimmie has been wonderful! You had great taste in girlfriends, son, and I'm so glad you brought her into our lives. I wish you were here, but since you're not, I'm glad you left us your friends.

It's been almost four months since you were killed and the man who killed you finally has a case number. But now I can't get the State's attorney to return my calls.

September 30th (Day 116)

The neighbor kids were playing football in the street yesterday, and I began to cry. It's the little things that often bring the tears. I hate having to give up the vitality and life that you brought to my world . . . it feels so bland and void without you.

You've been dead four months and it seems as though life has gone on without being affected, as though everyone has forgotten you. Yet, Bonnie (my friend from work) said that ever since your death, she wears her seat belt. Maybe the impact of your death is so widespread and subtle that I will never know it. If I could only know the impact your death had on others, I believe I could bear losing you more easily.

October 2nd (Day 118)

Gentle spirit hovering above
touch me sweetly
with your soul
and place a gentle kiss
on my heart.

October 3rd (Day 119)

I've finally talked to the State Solicitor's Office and found out that the young man who was driving the car that killed you has a long list of traffic violations, including another accident and other failures to yield. I'm livid! If he had paid significant consequences for previous violations, maybe you'd be alive. Justice! This life has none!

October 4th (Day 120)

I know my son is in heaven, Lord.
I know my child is with you.
I know you are caring for him, Lord,
but what is a mother to do?
My arms reach out to hold him.
My hands long to touch him once more.
My eyes just long to see him.
My heart is constantly sore.
My life is so lonesome without him.
My dreams are no longer there.
My plans have withered and dried,
but my soul still longs to share.

October 6th (Day 122)

We went to your grave again yesterday to bring fresh flowers. We do that weekly. Do you know that? Of course you do. At least, I hope you do.

I always get so sad when I go out there. On a day-to-day basis I talk to you through my heart, no matter where I am. But when I go to your grave, the reality of your body lying in that ground hits me flat in the face, and I don't like it. No matter how much faith I have that your heart and soul live on, my mother's heart is torn by the thought of your beloved, broken body lying in that gray box.

♥ ♥ ♥

The searing pain is gone now. I'm no longer doubled over by my grief, but the dull, constant ache is still there. I talk about you daily, and I've needed to do that, but I think that need is changing. I think it's time to softly tuck your memory into my heart and realize that, even though you will always be a part of me, you are no longer an active part of my daily existence, and that hurts.

Son, my precious only son, life has never demanded as much from me as it has these past months. It will be four months tomorrow since you were snatched from me. In fact, four months ago today, you were still alive and real. You were at the beach, working on your tan. Why, oh why, oh why were you taken?

October 16th (Day 132)

Today we go to court. Today is the day the young man who caused your death is scheduled to make his plea. Once his plea is entered, Dad and I will have a chance to talk before the judge.

How am I going to feel when I see the young man who took your life? I don't know. Right now I feel a little numb, and I'm just proceeding on a "do what I have to do" basis. I feel as though I've been functioning on that level ever since you died.

It's so exhausting for me to replay the night of your death in my mind, and that is exactly what happens when I think of that young man.

I miss you, my Rob, and I wish I didn't have to go to court today or that I'd never heard of the young man who will be there, but that's not reality. So, please help me make it through this painful reality; be with me in that courtroom and help me to be the mother you were proud of: the strong, gentle, sure, and open Mom.

October 17th (Day 133)

We did go to court yesterday, and I was all prepared to speak before the judge. But my chance didn't come—at least not yet. The young man had been arraigned on Monday! The solicitor (State's Attorney) had given me the wrong date.

It was so awful. Dad, Kim and I were so psyched up to handle this thing—to see the man who killed you—then chillingly cold water was dashed into our faces, and we hit the bottom of the emotional roller coaster we have been riding on.

When no one showed up as we had expected them to, we had to track down what was happening. I wanted to cry, scream, and rage. I was hurting badly. Didn't people know how necessary it was for me to be kept abreast of this case? This young man, because of his choice and his mistake, took the life of my son. I need to see him—to see what kind of person he is—to know what consequence he will pay. Are all of the people who handle these cases so detached from their feelings that they aren't aware of the pain that we (the victims) are going through? Or is this a pain you know about only after you feel it? I don't know. I just know that yesterday I relived a lot of the emotional exhaustion caused by your death.

But Kim, Dad, and I pulled together. We had lunch after we left the courthouse, and Kimmie wanted to have Krystal hamburgers. You remember how she loves those silly square little burgers? Well, it was an experience, let me tell you! But it brought laughter because I'm such a veggie lover and semi health nut...so eating at Krystal's was a new experience for me. And we needed the laughter.

After lunch we drove around looking at houses, then we went to the "Show of Homes" and looked at dream houses. We made it a good day.

October 25th (Day 141)

Last night was such a great night. Dad, Rica and her mom Sheila, and Kim and her mom Sharon, and I went to see *The Phantom of the Opera* at the Fox Theater. It was fabulous! You probably wouldn't have been crazy about it, but we loved it!

To top off the night, the Braves won another game in the World Series. They creamed the Twins, 14-5. The headlines in the paper this morning read "Sakes Alive – 14-5!" It was great! The Fox Theater was packed for the *Phantom* performance and during intermission people were listening to the Braves' game on their radio headsets. With every run the Braves made, the crowd would roar and start doing the Tomahawk Chop! I loved it!

I wonder what you think about all this. I mean, the Braves versus the Twins. Georgia (the state you loved) versus Minnesota (the state you grew up in). What a year of history-making events: Atlanta got the Olympics, the Braves get into the World Series, and I lost my son—joy and pain all tumbled together like clothes in a dryer in this life-affecting year.

October 26th (Day 142)

We went to Ed's parents' house for dinner last night. We had a great time. Maybe we'll be able to become friends with them. I hope so.

Were you and Ed with us last night? Were you both there enjoying the fact that we had so much in common with his parents and that you and Ed were so much alike? God works in mysterious ways. He brought us together through the loss of our sons. Was this one of His wonders? I don't know, but maybe we can help each other. I hope so—to think of any human being suffering the kind of emotional pain that I've endured is hard to handle.

Yesterday in the mail, I received a subpoena to the court case for the young man whose actions killed you. It is going to be on November 25th. That's the Monday we had planned to be at my sister Kathy's home. Of all the days it could have been scheduled, why that one? Who knows? I just know it is. Now, once more, I'll get all emotionally psyched up for this thing. I hope I'm not dashed against sharp rocks again.

November 20th (Day 167)

I called the State Solicitor's Office to check on the case for Monday. Good thing I did. The hearing has been postponed again, and no one in the State Solicitor's Office bothered to let me know. Maybe death is so much a part of their work that they don't even think about the pain of the survivors.

At least we can go to my sister's home for Thanksgiving. I need family this first Thanksgiving without you.

November 26th (Day 173)

We're at your Aunt Kathy's home for Thanksgiving again this year. I keep remembering the trip last year when you came with us. I had no idea it would be our last Thanksgiving together. Shouldn't a mother know? Shouldn't we have this innate knowledge about our children? How can God give us the ability to hurt so badly at the loss of a child without giving us something with which we can balance, that hurt? Or does He give us a balance and I just don't see it right now?

My half-brother Brian came over to Kathy's house yesterday, and he and Dad went off and spent some time together. Dad is responding to children and young people better than he ever has. Losing you has impacted our lives in so many ways. I know we'll feel the ripples of that loss forever, but right now we are often being overwhelmed with the waves of pain.

I've started my Christmas shopping, and it's very difficult because I see things you would enjoy. Such a large part of my life has been lost that I sometimes wander around in a gray fog not recognizing what's left.

I've even distanced some from your sister. I'm not sure why, and I don't even know if she recognizes that I have. But deep inside of me a door to my inner heart and soul has been locked. Maybe it's just temporary, maybe it's not. I just know that there is a wounded inner part that nobody really understands or knows how to respond to. So, for now, I'll close it away and protect it. Because if that part of me got damaged, even unknowingly, it would bleed the will to live right out of me.

My sister, Darlene, took me to the Precious Moments Chapel in Carthage, Missouri, yesterday. It was created by Samuel Butcher, the man who created the Precious

Moments figurines. The chapel is filled with paintings and stained glass windows depicting scenes from the Bible where the characters are all represented by "Precious Moment" figurines. He has one painting of heaven from a child's view. It's a scene at the pearly gates where a child is being welcomed to heaven. Were there a lot of people there to welcome you, Rob? I know you were there to welcome Ed, and the two of you are doing something special up there. It's probably unorthodox, and you're probably giving God gray hair and stretching Him to grow as much as God can. At least, that's how I imagine it because that was your effect on me. You constantly looked at life differently than I did and approached it from a different angle. In doing so, you made it necessary for me to be more open-minded. I miss that. I miss the challenge and knowledge you brought to my life. Let's face it, I miss you, kiddo. From the very depths of my heart, I miss you.

November 29th (Day 176)

The Thanksgiving weekend has had its pain. The tears just kept flowing, and I really felt pulled in and wounded. I know I wasn't a lot of fun to be around and I'm not sure that surrounding myself with family for the Holidays is such a good idea. They see my pain and they hurt, which diminishes their enjoyment of the occasion.

Oh poop, Rob, there just is no logical or simple way through this hell called grief. There is no easy 1-2-3-step plan to help a parent get over the death of a child. I believe I'm doing all the "healthy" things: feeling my feelings, not stuffing the pain, going on with my life, etc., but all those things still don't make it easy, and I tremble at the thought of it being harder.

I still want to scream, "It's not fair! It's not fair! The young man who killed my Rob is spending Thanksgiving with his family. He can still plan a future and look forward to getting married and having a family. My Rob can't!"

I don't diminish for one moment that your life in heaven is sweet, and that God has special plans for you; I just haven't figured out how in the hell I can let go of your future down here. I still want to scream and moan, "Not my Rob, please, not my Rob! I can handle anything, but please don't take my children, and please, oh please, oh please, not my Rob!" Then I want to drop on my knees and say "God, why did you take my Rob? Why are you punishing me? What did I do to deserve this pain?"

Logically, I know God isn't trying to hurt me and that He's here helping me through this, but emotionally I get absolutely buried in the pain and agony of going ahead without you. It's almost like abandoning one of my children. How can I do that? Sometimes I feel so stuck in this place— this hole—where I lost you. Then at other times, I grasp on to my dreams and the people surrounding me, and go on with my life, even gleefully.

Today I feel better than yesterday. But why? Why should one day, just because we call it a holiday, be ever so much more painful than the day after or the day before? It's the memories in our minds. We have set aside our memories of holidays into this special little place, and we remember them so explicitly whereas the daily memories of a lifetime get all jumbled together.

One more milestone in the rest of my life, Rob; I've survived Thanksgiving without you, my beautiful son. And I'll survive every day and every holiday on earth that God grants me. I just don't know what damage the surviving does to my wounded, beaten, and frail mother's heart.

December 8th (Day 185)

Happy twenty-first birthday my son!

My heart is full of pain this morning as I think of all the plans we would have had, and how you had looked forward to coming of age. I'm trying to dwell on the day you were born instead of the day you died.

We've invited Kim and the neighbors over to have champagne and the Banana Split Cake that you loved. I don't know where your soul is—here with us or off on a higher plane that we cannot understand. Wherever you are, Happy Birthday, my precious son. I miss you with all my heart, and I love you!

December 9th (Day 186)

Well Rob, yesterday was a day of many emotional ups and downs . . . tears, anger, sadness, then excitement and hope. The tears flowed all day as I remembered the day you were born and all of the twenty birthdays we celebrated together.

Pastor Holly came and brought over the plant we had purchased for the Sunday service at the church in your memory. I felt sadness, yet thankfulness that people like Holly care.

I have mixed feelings about the gathering we had in remembrance of your birthday. I wanted to talk about happy memories of you, and it didn't come off. It's as if everybody worked hard to change the subject, and I felt angry. I get so tired of people trying to decide for me how I should grieve. I am a healthy, intelligent woman, and between me and God, we'll figure out what I need. I don't need somebody else doing that. I know they are well-intending, but I hate it when people shuffle away from talking about you as if by doing so I won't think about you or have any pain. How stupid! I'm going to have pain, period! And not dealing with it is just going to keep the pain inside where it can fester.

I'm not about to turn myself into a victim where all I do is walk around talking about you and my pain. I don't do that! I function very well on a daily basis, but on particularly painful days—holidays, your birthday, etc.—I need to walk right through the mouth of the pain and face it head on so that it doesn't sneak up behind me and consume me.

My biggest frustration is that those people close enough (geographically) to be with me during these times can't seem to let me face my pain. Are they so terrified that they could lose one of their children that they can't stand to see my hurt? Or is all of this within me and has nothing to do with them? There doesn't seem to be a way that people really can win when someone is grieving, because we're all so different. There is no answer except to be aware of the person in grief and take your clues from them. I wish more people were doing that for me. I did get calls from my sisters—Kathy, Darlene, and Beverly—and I talked to my mom.

A lady whose daughter is buried not too far from you called me. She said the balloons and flowers we put on your grave let her know that it was your birthday, and she wanted me to know she knows exactly where I'm at. It's so sad that we have to lose a child to really understand the pain.

December 24th (Day 201)

Well, here we are, son, my first Christmas Eve without you since you were born, twenty-one years ago. Days, months, years just keep creeping past me, seemingly oblivious to the demand that living is exacting on me right now.

The box of gifts that we shipped from Atlanta to California to Grandma and Grandpa's house isn't here. We'll have Christmas with just the presents from them that are under the tree. It's childish and stupid, but I want to stomp my feet and scream, "I don't need this! No more changes, let everything else be okay, perfect! Lori's not here, my grandson Christopher's not here, Rob's not here, that's all I can handle—my life is absent."

Except for Chuck who is always here, always dependable, yet sometimes the cause of my pain. He shipped the gifts— he sent them standard air—never thinking to check if that was enough time. I want to scream at him, beat my fist against his chest, and tell him it's his fault I'm having a lousy Christmas!

But it's not his fault that you're gone. Is my anger his fault? Am I still internally railing at him that the two of you weren't closer? You were close, just not by my mother's standards that would have created a world where you both hugged a lot and where you shared your deepest thoughts with him. I know ... that's not how guys relate! But I wanted a perfect world for you, and I'm angry at Chuck that he kept it from being perfect. I'm hiding behind rose-colored glasses trying to believe that any world can be perfect.

I went in and lay down on the bed early this evening and just let the tears flow. I felt so empty without you or Lori ... my children, my life. Pain ebbed from every pore, but in Grandma and Grandpa's house I didn't feel that the signs of pain were okay because then it would be tangible where they'd have to look at it and perhaps acknowledge their own pain, which I don't think they have yet.

Grandma made dinner and everything kept on schedule in their world while mine was tilting, and a horrible screaming siren was going off inside my head as if to warn me that to go any farther in this imbalance would cause me irreparable harm. But life gives me no choice. It requires that I continue on, even in my state of extreme imbalance.

When I sat down at the table, my tears returned, turning into small, silent sobs as I tried to keep them contained. Their strength ripped me apart inside as I tried to keep them caged. Their intensity was magnified within the confines of my heart and soul, whereas if they'd been exposed to the outside and other people's compassion, they would have shrunk to trickles of tears and sadness.

I covered my face with my hands and mumbled an apology. Not a word was spoken. I know they cared, but without verbal confirmation, I was bereft of the knowledge of their concern.

I don't know if leaving home this Holiday was a good decision or if I was trying to run from pain that was inevitable. But, this Christmas—like so many things in life—came with no rehearsals or second chances. So, I'll just have to live with the results of my choices and realize it was an imperfect situation in an imperfect life.

December 31st (Day 208)

We're home, Rob, and it was a bittersweet holiday. We visited places you lived when you were young, went sliding in Nevada on the hill you used to love, and spent time with kids you used to play with. The memories swam in my mind. The laughter and tears mingled together like a heavy blanket of pine needles—warm, but with many sharp points that pierced tender areas.

♥ ♥ ♥

People say I talk about you like you're still here. Don't they know that you are still an important part of my life? Your spirit, your memories, your impact on me, are always there. Am I to tuck your name away in the dark attic of my life and relish the memories and sweetness of your existence in solitary hours, never sharing them with others because it makes them uncomfortable?

To this I say, "Tough!" I have never been able to give to life the conformities that it seems to demand. I've always responded in the way that seemed natural to me. It's been my misfortune (or fortune, depending upon my perspective at the moment) that this doesn't meet the rules of conformity or normalcy that people in my life seem to think exists.

The trip exhausted me beyond measure as I tried to deal with the difference between "normal" people and myself. The "normals" seem to feel that feelings or emotions are to be stuffed and controlled. I think they are to be felt and experienced, while always being sensitive to those around me.

The "normals" seem to feel that the past is something to be stuffed in the background and ignored, especially if it contains any pain. I believe the past is a mirror on which we reflect the visions and dreams of our future.

January 4th (Day 212)

My anger came out again today...surging, screaming and clawing its way up through my body. These tiny ripples of pain that bubble and gurgle deep inside of me . . . the pain of loss and loneliness . . . never seem to go away or find a venting or an avenue of release, even in communication.

Grief is tough on our marriage because we are grieving so differently. I understand why some marriages don't make it through a loss like this. Will we? My answer would change, depending on the day and time you asked me that question.

Today while I was putting away the Christmas decorations I lovingly fingered the ornament you made for me in either kindergarten or first grade. It has your picture in the center with a dough wreath surrounding it. Love folded its arms around me, then rage smashed me to the ground. "Why? Why? Why? Why my Rob?" Will that question never go away? It has gone away from my mind, quenched with logical answers and Christian beliefs, but my heart often breaks through in totally primal pain— yelling, screaming, and raging, "I don't understand! I don't accept! It's not okay!" As if that will change things, make them better, but it doesn't.

Just yesterday I realized that since we are now in a new year, you died last year. Last year—should that have some significance as to the amount of pain I have? It doesn't. The amount is still overwhelming. It just doesn't occur as often. Perhaps that's what preserves my sanity.

I am a sensible, smart woman who continues in life with her own plans and dreams. I put energies into those around me that I choose to have in my life. My days are full. Yet, always down in the farthest corner of my heart, pain lurks—always ready to come to the surface—ever threatening to erupt.

Son, oh my son,
I miss you.
I'll always miss you.
Life, days, years
will never take that away.

January 9th (Day 217)

It's been a tough week. The young man whose car killed you has been due in court this week. First we went to the courthouse Tuesday morning expecting a trial, only to have it postponed. So Dad and I headed back to our offices, and by the time I got to mine, I had a call from the State Solicitor's Office—the young man was going to submit a plea on Thursday and we'd get a chance to talk to the judge. This was it. All these months and I was finally going to get to see him, and he was finally going to pay a penalty for taking your life.

I didn't sleep last night—I kept going over and over in my mind what I wanted to say to the judge and how I wanted to say it. Well, I finally got to say it. I finally got to see the young man, and it was anticlimactic. He was a young man who was suffering, scared, yet belligerent. I could see it in his eyes. I don't believe he fully comprehends what he has done. He's young, and youth protects us from the full harshness of life. He's probably never lost anyone. He can't know the pain, and he really doesn't seem to be in touch with what paying consequences means. He plea bargained ahead of time and knew he was going to lose his license, yet he drove, by himself, to the courthouse. The judge asked the bailiff to make sure that he did not leave the premises behind the wheel of a car. For that I was very thankful.

The judge also ordered him to pay restitution to us. I will be really surprised if that transpires. His actions killed a man—they killed you—but he doesn't seem to realize what he's done. He will someday, and that's the day my prayers will be with him—he'll need them.

It was good to be able to show your picture and finally speak my thoughts in front of the young man who caused your death. This is what I said:

"Your Honor, during these proceedings this morning, we have all had an opportunity to put a face to the name of the young man who has been charged in this case. I would now like to do that for my son, Rob, by showing a picture of him to the State, the Court and the young man and his attorney, as I believe it is very important that everyone involved in this case be able to visually conceptualize what my husband and I have lost.

"Your Honor, I am not an angry, vindictive woman. I am a caring, compassionate woman who knows that mistakes and accidents do happen. And if I believed that my son's death was just that, I would not be before you today and the young man sitting here would have my forgiveness and my prayers. However, your Honor, I am familiar with his driving record:

"Eight years ago -   Ran a red light or stop sign
Seven years ago -   Improper Lane change which
                      resulted in an accident
Three years ago -   Ran a red light or stop sign and a
                      few months later, a DUI
Two years ago -   Another traffic violation of which I
                      do not have the details

"And on June 7th of last year, a Failure to Yield which resulted in the death of my son. At 9:21 p.m. on June 7th, my son was a vibrant, beautiful young man with the potential of a full and wonderful life ahead of him. At 9:22 p.m., because of this young man's decision not to yield (for whatever reason), my son's body lay on the pavement. Every major bone in his body was broken; he suffered from severe brain damage and, for all intents and purposes, was dead at that moment.

"My son had no choice in whether he died that day. I had

no say in a circumstance that has caused me gut-wrenching pain and one which took the life of my only son. This is a loss that I will live with for the rest of my life. This young man sitting here today, however, did have a choice when he decided not to yield. And it is my fervent wish, Your Honor, that he understand the results of that choice and that the impact create an awareness and sense of responsibility in him that he will never again have a traffic violation or have to appear before any court. I want my son's death to not have been in vain."

After I was done talking, I handed your picture to the bailiff, who handed it to the judge. The judge looked at your photo for several moments and then passed it to the young man's attorney, stating that we wanted his client to see it. That young man was very still as he held your photo; I believe that reality hit him hard for that moment in time.

Then it was your dad's turn to talk. He was very eloquent today and passion crept into his voice as he talked. I saw just a tiny bit of the pain he has suffered. I think he has stuffed it so deep inside, he hasn't even felt it yet.

It was after Dad and I spoke that the judge said the case had been plea bargained so he was not able to change the penalty, but he could add restitution payable to us, which he did. At the end of the proceedings, the judge gave us his condolences. He said he had teenagers and he didn't know what he would do if he lost them.

Pastors Dave and Holly met us at the courthouse. It was so nice to have them there. It was a hard day for all of us and especially for Kimmie. This has been a tough year for her. At just eighteen, she has learned a lot about the hardness of life.

Chapter 2

Trying to Move On

January 13th (Day 221)

Now that the young man who caused your death has been
meted his punishment and the courts have done their job . . .
or did they . . . I should be able to "turn the page" and move
forward, but it's not easy. Grieving is full of many sharp
turns and curves, and they often catch me off-balance like
they did yesterday.

I had a terrible day. Loneliness and sadness hung heavily
around my neck, making me morose and angry. Every time
I turned around, you were in my thoughts, and not the good
memories—the hard ones. An ambulance passed us, and I
began to cry. And tears gushed from my eyes as I walked
through the floral department at the grocery store because
I know that the most I can now do for you is to put fresh
flowers on your grave. Then Dad and I were cleaning out
the cabinet below the fish tank and I found some of your
college-related paperwork as well as a note you had written
to us a few months before you died, and I began to cry.

All day long pain seeped through every pore of me, leaving

me feeling hopeless and as though this aching will never be better. If I had to deal with it at this intensity for any extended period of time, I couldn't take it. I feel so terribly beaten down and exhausted from the whole process. But I have to remember that was yesterday, and not every day has been like that. As my sister Kathy said, it takes longer and longer for the pressure to build up under my emotions now. I have to remember that, and not be hard on myself, but to gently love myself through one more step.

Why did it all happen, Rob? Why? Sure, we can put all kinds of rational answers to that question as well as we can come up with all of the logical steps to grieving, but this is not a logical experience. Losing you was a heavily emotional experience, one that tore through the very heart of me, racing past my mind and ignoring its attempt to try to put this into a box of orderly feelings and experiences. There is no box that my sadness and grief will fit into. It bounces off the walls of my pain and logic to reverberate around my heart.

January 14th (Day 222)

I once had a son who wore his cap like that,
the brim to the back and the thin plastic adjusting band
on his forehead, over his fine, blond hair.

A son whose intense blue eyes
spoke of the dreams, ideas and plans
that jogged around in his mind.

A son whose future was bright because of
his intelligence, his ambition and his ability
to love without judgment.

I once had a son who wore his cap like that.

A son who loved motorcycles and wanted one of his own.
We wouldn't give in. I'm good on a motorcycle, Mom,
he'd plead.

It's the other guy you have to watch out for, his father
would warn.

I once had a son who wore his cap like that.

He'd often borrow motorcycles from his friends
and go for rides.

It helps me clear my mind, he'd say.
One day while he was
clearing his mind,
a car pulled out in front of him.

I once had a son who wore his cap like that.

January 25th (Day 233)

My anger has been strong again lately. It's not focused anger. I'm not angry at God, or at the young man whose actions killed you. I'm angry at everything! I'm angry that life goes on, and I'm angry that yours didn't.

When you first died, I tried to fill our lives with other young people, but it's not the same. They aren't you. That horrible hole that's been left in my life will never be filled, and that hurts!

People lie when they say time heals. It doesn't. Maybe the pain doesn't come as frequently, but when it comes, it's just as strong. I miss your love, Rob. That faith and trust and sometimes adoration that you and Lori had for me doesn't come from anywhere else. And the bond that was between us was like nothing else I've ever experienced. I feel so damned angry that I've lost it with you!

I'm realistic enough to know that when something is lost, all focus goes to it. And I know I still have my husband Chuck, my daughter Lori, my grandson Christopher and Lori's new baby who will soon be here...and for them I'm grateful. But what do I do with the loneliness I have for you? How do I fill that or temper it? I don't think I can. I think I'll just have to learn to live with it.

On the way to work yesterday I saw a guy in a brown leather jacket on a motorcycle. Immediately my mind started playing out the scene of your body flying through the air, hitting the car, and lying still—ever so still—on the ground. I can't seem to let go of that awful vision. One part of my mind can't stand it, and the other part is curious as to what it was like for you and if your spirit raised out of your body then (since I'm told you were brain dead on impact) or did your spirit stay in your body until you were actually dead at the hospital?

It's all these thoughts that visit me that make it hard for me to place you in the back of my mind and life. There is a part of me that refuses to put you there. That part rebels at the meaninglessness of life—we live, we die, we're forgotten. If so, why did we live in the first place?

January 27th (Day 235)

Dad called me at work yesterday to say that your marker had been placed. I felt like someone had knocked all the air out of me. I cried and couldn't get the tears to go very far away. They stayed right at the edge of my eyes all day.

Well, today we stopped by your grave, and there in writing it stated the day you were born and the day you died. I hate it, I hate it! I hate it! I sat on the ground and cried. It's in writing now. It's so much harder to ignore. That little piece of ground that I've been visiting for almost eight months now has your name on it! I thought it would be easier if we waited to get the marker. Well, I don't know if it was easier, I just know it wasn't easy.

The other day on the way to work I was thinking that before long summer would be here and it will be one year since you died, and then another and another and another, and I'll never get to see you again . . . at least not here on earth. Is acceptance of that supposed to come easier with time? Sure, I'm accepting it. What choice do I have? None! But, I don't like it! I'll never like it!

I miss you, son. What do I do with that? How do I ease the pain of the hole that was filled by your smile, your sense of humor, your energy for life? There is no other person in my life who is like you. You drove me crazy sometimes, but you challenged me into growth. Not only did you learn from me, you taught me.

What would you say to me now? What logical, philosophical statement would you come up with? I need to hear one. I can't always remember what your voice sounded like and that scares me. I don't want to forget that.

February 13th (Day 252)

Anger is a secondary emotion, I'm told. Well, my primary emotion is gut-wrenching loneliness . . . for my son, for life, for myself. It's as if when you died, Rob, any sense of who I am or where I'm going died with you. There is still that small part that hangs onto my dreams, but it flails against the sharp daggers of life, coming away with bleeding, open gashes. Who am I? Where am I going now that my mothering is over? I should be dealing with "empty nest syndrome," with you off in college and making your own life, not with your body lying in a cold, wintry grave.

I've felt so sad, lost and lonely for the past eight months (it feels like an eternity) that I don't know what other feelings feel like. Happy? Silly? Glad? Hopeful? What do those feel like?

When I met with Pastor Dave today I told him I feel abused, and maybe it's all the old hopelessness that goes with abuse. It feels like the bad times just go on and on. Yet, I know it's not all bad. I come home at night to a comfortable, loving home. It doesn't have the energy flowing through it now the way it did when you were alive, but it's a good place to be.

Maybe it's easier to go through grief without faith. Then I wouldn't expect anything. Maybe because I know God's power and because I believe in miracles, I expect too much. When He didn't come through the way I wanted, I'm having a hard time forgiving Him.

February 23rd (Day 262)

I've been dealing with a ghastly depression, Rob. It started about two weeks ago and very insidiously pulled me into its depths. The pain of losing you seemed stronger than it was in the beginning. Stress from work pulled at me from one side and the stress of depression pulled at me from the other. I felt like I was going crazy. It got so bad that on Thursday night all I did was cry. Finally I called Brian at work on Friday morning and told him that when I left work on Thursday, I had every intention of giving them my notice. He talked with me a long time. He said that what I'm going through is normal, that I will have peaks and valleys; to take care of myself when I feel the valleys coming.

So Dad and I went away for the weekend. We rented this little cabin in the boondocks of the Georgia mountains. We haven't turned on a television or radio since we got here. We've talked, slept, and relaxed. Yesterday we went horseback riding. That was fun! I kept thinking of you and how you'd probably call it a sissy ride, but it was so great! We went off on this trail and galloped some and cantered some.

I felt so giddy I wanted to giggle. One of the other horses took off with a young girl on it. She handled it well. Had it been me, my jeans would have been damp on the way back! The other horses also got a little antsy, and when mine started dancing around a bit my heart went thumpedty-thump-thump. I pulled hard on the reins a couple of times, and he behaved himself. Thank goodness!

My horse's name was "Jazz," and he's a good old horse. I'd like to come up again and ride him, maybe bring Kim and Rica.

I've been thinking about that, too, how I seem to want to give enjoyment to everyone else instead of concentrating on me and taking care of me. I'm not even sure what makes me feel good. The darndest thing is that at my age, I don't seem to know a lot about me anymore. Yet I know more about myself than a lot of people seem to know about themselves. That's a bit of a puzzle, isn't it?

Sometimes I'm not sure what part of this pain is grief and how much of it is "empty nest syndrome" or "mid-life crisis." Everything in my life is turned upside down. When I get as depressed and angry as I was, I don't stay in touch with God, and when that happens, I feel really lost.

I was furious with God underline! Furious that He intentionally took you away from me, or if not, He didn't do a miracle to save you. So, either way, He was responsible for my loss and pain, and that for me was not acceptable behavior from a Heavenly Father who's supposed to love me.

Another thing I was really ticked about was all the clichés and pat answers that people kept giving me: "Time heals," etc. That doesn't do one darn thing to ease the crazy-making pain that I'm in right now.

This weekend when we had gotten away from the city and its busyness, the verse: "You've got to walk that lonesome valley, you've got to walk it by yourself, nobody else can walk it for you, you've got to walk it by yourself," kept going through my mind. I guess if only I can walk it, then I'd better concentrate on taking care of me.

I'm learning, Rob, each horribly painful step of the way . . . I'm learning.

Life goes on. We live, we laugh, we have fun. But where are you?

February 25th (Day 264)

I seem to have shut you and the depression out—away from me. I am forcing myself to write in my journal daily, or as close to it as I can maintain.

Grief is confusing. Books tell me one thing and then every person I meet has their own advice or input which varies as extremely as their life's experiences differ. I'm so frustrated by it all that I want to put my hands over my ears and scream, "Leave me alone!" On top of all this depression and emotional pain, I'm not feeling well physically, and I don't know if it's caused from my depression or vice versa—which came first, the chicken or the egg?

It's hard to write when I'm shut down; at least, I think I'm shut down. I'm not sure. I just know I feel exhausted and drained of feelings.

Last night I looked at your picture and didn't cry. That was an achievement! I have to remember, however, that doesn't mean I'll be able to do that tomorrow. That's what I need to accept: my days and feelings are not and will not be predictable. This is a one-step, one-day-at-a-time process. I've never been good at going through the process. I'm a bottom-line kind of gal. I know people are well-meaning with their advice, prognosis and judgments, but they are driving me crazy! Somehow, I need to be able to let it all slide off my back, retaining only the suggestions that might work for me.

February 25th (Day 264)

I seem to have shut you and the depression out—away from me. I am forcing myself to write in my journal daily, or as close to it as I can maintain.

Grief is confusing. Books tell me one thing, and then every person I meet has their own advice or input which varies as extremely as their life's experiences differ. I'm so frustrated by it all that I want to put my hands over my ears and scream, "Leave me alone!" On top of all this depression and emotional pain, I'm not feeling well physically, and I don't know if it's caused from my depression or vice versa—which came first, the chicken or the egg?

It's hard to write when I'm shut down; at least, I think I'm shut down. I'm not sure. I just know I feel exhausted and drained of feelings.

Last night I looked at your picture and didn't cry. That was an achievement! I have to remember, however, that doesn't mean I'll be able to do that tomorrow. That's what I need to accept: my days and feelings are not and will not be predictable. This is a one-step, one-day-at-a-time process. I've never been good at going through the process. I'm a bottom-line kind of gal. I know people are well-meaning with their advice, prognoses and judgments, but they are driving me crazy! Somehow, I need to be able to let it all slide off my back, retaining only the suggestions that might work for me.

February 29th (Day 268)

Rob, where are the really honest books about grieving...
the ones that talk about the hideous valleys of depression,
loneliness, and hopelessness? Are there books written
by mothers who talk about the fight within themselves
between the intellectual, the spiritual, and the mother's
heart? Where are all these books? The writer in me wants
books I can relate to, books that can help me find my own
answers. Where are they?

I'm so tired of the clichés: "Time heals . . . It will get
better . . ." Bullshit! I'll have to live with the pain. It won't
get better! Maybe it won't come as often, but I'll never
completely heal! How can having a child ripped out of your
life ever "get better"? And why do people think they have to
deliver these clichés and platitudes? I know that the people
around me feel helpless as they watch me struggle in dark
pits of despair, but when someone is bleeding to death, do
you toss him a bandage from the sidelines, or do you get
close, hold them, and apply as much pressure to the wound
as you can to help stop the drain of life-giving blood?

I know I don't make it easy. I know I close people out, but
I don't know how to do this grieving thing. Why haven't I
attended a "Compassionate Friends" or similar group? I'm
not sure. Right now I feel as though maybe it's time I just
shut off my mind and words about you. Maybe if I refuse to
talk about you, or think about you, maybe if I pack all your
pictures away, this gloom and depression will leave me. Do
I want to pay that kind of price? I'm not sure...that's a big
price to pay.

Why would God do such a thing? Why would He deprive
me of one of the most precious things in my life? Didn't I
deserve you? Didn't I take good enough care of you? That
can't be it, because there are thousands of abused children

who live until they're old. So why, Rob, why? Does He have a purpose for you up there? That doesn't help me down here. And . . . if that's the case, why is He letting me hurt so badly? Or is it me? Am I somehow doing this wrong? Is there a right or a wrong way to grieve?

March 23rd (Day 290)

I can't go to church anymore . . . not right now. I sit there and stare at the front, and all I see is your coffin. My mind haunts and torments me every day, but on Sundays, it's merciless. And I don't feel close to God right now. I don't know what I feel or who I feel it for. I'm numb, empty, and drained of all my reasons for living.

April 4th (Date 302)

Dad and I stopped by your grave today, and I sat there, surrounded by the ducks, looking at the lake, and crying. Will the crying ever stop? Will the pain ever completely leave? I don't think so. I think there will be a part of me that always cries at my loss. I'm able to function better now. I am slowly but surely proceeding with my life, whatever that may be at the moment. But I still hurt—deeply.

I asked Dad if he thought the pain would ever end. He just shook his head and said, "I don't know." I think he's finally dealing with it, Rob. He has suffered as much, if not more than I have, but he's done it so differently, and that in itself has been difficult on our marriage. It's hard to understand our own grief, let alone someone else's when they respond so differently.

Anger used to be my first response to Dad when he wouldn't talk about his pain or when he seemed so in control, now I just feel compassion and sadness because I know he's hurting—maybe not in a way I can identify with, but he's hurting. And in some ways his hurt is even more intense because the two of you had not worked into the close relationship that you and I were working on. Dad and I both feel really ripped off because we didn't get a chance to have a relationship and friendship with Rob, the man. That part was just beginning, and it ended so abruptly. We will always have grief and a sense of loss over that.

April 25th (Day 323)

Dad was in the bedroom last night talking to Pedro, our Chihuahua, and he said "Hello" the way you used to. (Remember when you'd come in the front door and say "Hello?") My heart stopped for a moment as fantasy fought with reality. Reality won as my mind replayed spots of agony from these past eleven months . . . eleven months! How can that be? How can I have lived for eleven months after the death of my child?

I used to say that losing one of my children would kill me. I guess it hasn't. Maybe that would have been the easy way out.

May 10th (Day 338)

I'm beginning to hate holidays. This would have been just another Sunday where we went to church, maybe to breakfast, and then home. I would have thought of you some today the way I do every day, but today is Mother's Day, and that brought the pain of your loss screaming down against my heart. We went to church, out to breakfast and then stopped by your grave. I looked at the grass that is now completely grown over where your coffin lies deep within the ground, and I thought about one year ago. Back then, I had a son. Now, I don't. What else will life bring? Will Mother's Day ever come again without pain?

Holidays are made for happy people . . . for people whose lives have never been touched by pain. And I don't believe people like that exist. So, why do we keep having holidays? I truly think I hate them. At least, today I do.

May 26th (Day 354)

I go in spurts when I don't write because everything is relatively even in my life. Each day has little stresses, but my cup of grief isn't overflowing. Then, suddenly, it's flapping up in big, tumultuous waves again, and I need to journal.

What brings it from calm to hurricane conditions in seemingly one day's time? This time it started with Mother's Day, then Memorial Day, and the ever-lurking first anniversary of your death.

When the pain hits like this, it's still intense. It doesn't come often anymore, but when it does, it still knocks the wind out of me. And compassion from others now seems gone. Their attitudes seem to be: "It's time to let it go. It's time to get on with your life. Pick yourself up, give yourself a kick, and get over this."

These attitudes stick in my throat, choking the last breath from me. They seem to imply that I'm not doing those things and ninety percent of the time now, I am. But the other ten percent is still spent in the valleys of pain. Only other parents who have lost children seem to understand.

May 27th (Day 355)

Evie called me last night, Rob. Do you remember when she and Jack visited us in Texas? I worked for them when I was sixteen and seventeen years old and have kept in contact with them all through these years. They lost their son, Allen, when he was about eight. He died of Leukemia. Your middle name was in his memory.

Evie knows what I'm going through. She still suffers some and Allen has been dead for over twenty years. That's the reality of the death of a child– -it never goes away! That I can handle . . . that makes sense! How could it go away? How can people expect that it will?

Evie's love and compassion reached out to me through the telephone, and I felt nurtured. She loves me, she cares, she understands. What more could I ask for? Our talk didn't take the pain away, but it stilled the agony. And that's all that's necessary. The hard part is that Evie touches my life so seldom because she is so far away, and the people who touch my life daily don't offer the compassion and understanding I need. Do we all have to go through the same hideous pain in order to offer each other compassion, empathy, and love? I hope not. What a sad world this is, if that's the case.

I don't know what I want from others. I know what I don't want. I don't want them crowding me and telling me how to grieve and how long to do it. You weren't their son, you were mine. At times, even yet, I still have a horrible time facing the fact that you're gone.

I'm struggling with my faith, Rob. Faith has been an integral part of life for me, seemingly since birth, and now I am really struggling with the issue of trust. How can I "let go and let God," believing He has my best interest at heart? He let you die. He didn't do a miracle, and He has the power.

Why didn't He, if He loves me so much? I don't know, son. You're up there now. You've got an inside line...talk to me. I'm drowning in doubt and mistrust as I choke on pain and grief.

Lord, do you hear me?
Do you really care?
I used to believe you did,
But now . . .
now, I'm infected with doubt.

Could you love me
and take my son?
Could you have my
best interest in mind
and let him die?

I don't know.
I don't understand.
Maybe I'm not supposed to,
and that's the biggest
confusion of all.

May 29th (Day 357)

I'm going through another valley, and they really suck! My emotions are unstable, my thinking is unclear, my physical self is exhausted. I can't deal with stress, and work is piled with stress! How do I cope? Minute by minute is the only answer I can come up with.

I'm really glad Lori and the grandbabies are with us now. People say it adds extra stress. I disagree! I can get lost in the love from those grandbabies and separate from the despair. What a beautiful, natural cure!

I woke up this morning with a start. My mind had a vision of your body lying so still and so cold in that ground. I couldn't stand it! I wanted to race to that graveyard, dig up the soil with my bare hands, and hold you against me. I looked at my bed where just a year ago you lay on your stomach, your head on your hands, talking to me about dreams. You were warm and alive then. It is torturous when my mind grips tightly to the visions of your dead, cold body. How do I make them go away...these valleys of pain that exhaust me?

June 3rd (Day 362)

The stench of death hadn't left my nostrils and people were telling me I had to go on living. Why couldn't they understand that a part of me had to die first? The part that was your mother had to die. People will argue with this. "You will always be his mother." Yes, yes, I will, just like you will always be my son. But, I have to lay those two people to rest—the mother of Rob and Rob the son.

I have many more identities that I have to take up with again, and some new ones that I have yet to discover. I've often looked to others to help put an identity to myself. We all do that in one form or another, and I've placed a great deal of my energies into Terri the mother, Terri the wife, and Terri the career woman...and the list goes on.

What about Terri the person? Period! I don't know. I struggle, I grasp, I try to survive, and maybe understand and grow in the process. What about just being? I don't know how.

June 4th (Day 363)

Like in a fairytale, I closed myself behind invisible glass walls this last year. Walls that were impenetrable. There I sat behind the walls, angry that people didn't reach in.

I still don't excuse those people unwilling to make the extra effort to realize that I needed them more than ever... that if I pushed them away, it was imperative that they stay quietly close before they tried again. True friends put in all the effort that is needed. True friends are rare.

No, I don't make excuses for those people, but I forgive them. And I forgive myself for not being gentle with me... for expecting so much instead of just grieving.

I did fairly well considering the pressure that was placed on me—by myself and others. But I let some of me die, the spunky part, the part you and Lori loved...the part you could always count on to survive no matter what was going on in our lives.

Maybe that woman is not really dead. Maybe she's just stopped breathing for a while, and I can bring her back to life.

Who knows? I guess it's worth a try. I unwillingly lost you to death; there's no sense in willingly giving up myself.

June 5th (Day 364)

Dad and I are in Washington, DC, for a week. Dad has to work and I came because I don't want to be without him on the first anniversary of your death. That day is looming over me like a large, dark cloud.

Today, while Dad was working, I drove down to Fredricksburg, Virginia. It's the birthplace of George Washington. I had a pleasant time. I was really impacted by a small churchyard cemetery. I was wandering through, looking at the dates on the grave stones. I looked at one stone, quickly subtracted the dates in my head and realized the woman was only twenty-two when she died.

Then it hit me. I wondered if a hundred or a hundred-and-fifty years from now, people will be wandering through the cemetery where you're buried and think, "so young to die."

I realized, maybe for the first time, that your grave is truly your final resting place. I may move from Atlanta—in fact, I most likely will—but you won't. Your body, or the remains of it, will be there forever.

June 7th (Day 366)

This has been the longest, hardest year of my life, but it's over. That first dreadful year is over—the first birthday without you, the first Christmas, the first Mother's Day.

I always said it would kill me if one of my children died. Well, it didn't . . . at least, not all of me.

The way Dad and I spent this day seemed so fitting. We went to Arlington Cemetery, Kennedy's grave, the Tomb of the Unknown Soldier, and the Vietnam Wall. I had been to Arlington before, and had seen the rows and rows of graves, but this time, it was different. This time I thought about the parents who had suffered the way I have and the way I do, and I didn't feel so alone. There are a lot of women out there who understand, who perhaps react the same to platitudes and clichés as I do.

June 11th (Day 370)

One year ago today we buried you, Rob. Your body has been lying in the ground through four seasons: the heat of summer; the colorful, cool days of fall; the chill and ice of winter; the life-giving, refreshing rains of spring. Yet it's been like one season for me . . . a long, gray, cold winter.

I went to the doctor today. I haven't been feeling well. I'm impatient with myself; it has been a year! But my body, mind, and emotions will heal on their own timetable and can't be forced ahead by sheer determination.

The feelings and pain are different now. They aren't as acute, but I'm certainly not to the point of calm, unemotional acceptance. Does a mother get to that point?

I was surprised at how hard the 7th was for your friends and our neighbors. Everyone coped in their own way. Lori and the kids went with your friends to the beach, in your memory. Your friend, Joe, took care of dumping all the girls into the water. He said you weren't there, so somebody had to do it. Kimmie didn't go along. Her mom said she was pretty quiet all day.

Kim really loved you, Rob. You were very fortunate to know a love like that at such a young age. I pray God will bring another special young man into her life. She says men like you are rare.

On the 7th, our neighbor Eileen did a lot of baking— things you used to love—blueberry muffins and chocolate cake. And Sheila, Rica's mom, thought of you all day with laughter and with tears.

We've all made it through this year. At times, we weren't sure we would. I know the pain's not over yet. We're still alive, the critical stage has passed, but we're far from normal or healthy. I still cry. Sometimes in deep, aching sobs that come up from the pit of my stomach, or at other times soft, gentle sobs that barely escape from between my lips.

A year ago I started the process of saying goodbye to you. And I'll probably be in some stage of that process all my life until we say hello again in eternity.

June 15th (Day 375)

I haven't heard from anyone at church for a while. Have they given up on us or forgotten about us? Or are they as confused about what to do with grief as we are? Somehow, someday, I have to tell people to keep reaching in, to keep letting those in grief know they're thought about.

I need an anchor. Who can be my anchor? Dad can't. I won't let God be right now, and many of the people I thought were my friends have all but disappeared from my world. It's lonely in here. Won't somebody please reach in and let me know they care?

June 20th (Day 380)

Today we had a birthday party for your nephew, Christopher. It was his second birthday, and we had the party in the backyard. As we sat around in the lawn chairs talking and laughing, I thought back to over a year ago when a similar grouping of people sat back there.

It was not a happy time then. Ed was with us, and we were all reeling from the shock of your death. Now he's gone too. I realize that a year from now someone else could be missing—snatched away by death. The thought no longer gives me a painful, wrenching feeling. If that happens, we'll survive. We'll hurt, we'll cry, we'll change, but we will continue to go on in this maze called life until it's our turn to die and take that big step into eternity.

Such is life. To some questions there are no answers, for some things there are no reasons, for some happenings there is no comprehension. Such is life.

Chapter 3

The Healing Begins

June 21st (Day 381)

Somehow, over the last couple of days, I've changed. I don't know exactly what the change is, yet I feel comfortable with it. Everything in my life seems to have shifted one hundred eighty degrees, and the shift is okay with me.

Since your death, I no longer sweat the small stuff. Things I couldn't have handled a little over a year ago, now I handle. I've wizened and matured since your death. I'm no longer sure of my path in life . . . where I'm intended to go, what I'm intended to do. Now the uncertainty is okay. Somehow, in the last few days, everything has settled around me, giving me strength and solidity like the ground settling around a fencepost that is shoved uninvited beneath its surface. Finally realizing that the post isn't going away, the soil adjusts and settles around it. That's the way I'm feeling about the pain, uncertainty and questions of life. They won't go away. I just have to settle in around them.

Dad and I were in your pickup yesterday (it will always be your pickup) and were at a stoplight when a young man pulled up next to us on a motorcycle similar to the one on which you were killed. When the light turned green and he pulled away and ahead of us, I imagined it was you. I started to imagine a car pulling out and your body flying through the air—the vision that has haunted my mind this whole year. This time, I didn't fight it, I didn't hide from it, I didn't flinch. I let my mind play it out—totally. I know now it wasn't bad for you, because once your head slammed against that car, you were brain dead, and you felt no pain.

I can go on now. I can adjust to the changes in my life, the people that touch my life, the changes in me. I love you, I'll always love you, and by loving you, I've come more closely to what I'm created to be.

Life is such a puzzle with all its funny pointed, many-armed pieces. Sometimes it's really hard to find a spot for a particular piece to go, and when we try to force it, the whole puzzle is pushed out of shape. Patience is what it takes...patience and the understanding that life is going to fill out around us whether we like the picture or not.

August 12th (Day 433)

I'm not sure Dad and I are going to survive as a couple. There's been too much pain . . . pain through which we have pulled apart, not together. He thinks I should be totally done crying about losing you. I'd like to see him cry so I can know he hurts too. I just don't have the energy for a divorce right now.

My friend Eve, who lives in Nevada, talks to me about the idealistic version of marriage the way God created it to be...the way hers is. Life for me has never stayed within idoalistic guidelines. I need my Christian friends to talk with me about reality, my reality. Why does God allow such pain in my life, and why isn't He helping me bear it better? I beseech Him to help me handle this daily cup that overflows, but He's not listening.

September 10th (Day 462)

I wrote a letter to the judge last week, Rob. We haven't heard anything about the restitution from the young man who was responsible for your death. I'm not letting this case slip through the cracks! That young man has got to take responsibility for this!

Then this afternoon I received a call from the young man's probation officer. She said he is a nice young man. He's been paying his restitution, and she wishes her case load had more good examples like him. Maybe this has had a big impact on him after all.

December 26th (Day 569)

Christmas this year was filled with Lori and the babies. Christopher reminds me a lot of you, and Dad is totally smitten with Hillary. She has "pa pa" firmly wound around her little fingers.

Lori and I both shed tears of pain and joy as we talked about your life and death. This year, though, the house was filled with squeals of delight as the babies enjoyed Christmas.

Lori said I was very quiet and looked sad. I don't think the sadness will ever totally go away.

March 30th (Day 665)

Lori and the kids have moved back to Minnesota, Rob. She's going back to college. Our life is suddenly so quiet. It's just Dad and me. This is rather terrifying. I don't have the busyness of life with children to keep me occupied when I'm not at work. Now I've really got to face life with just Dad. May God help us, because I don't know if Dad and I even know each other anymore.

June 7th (Day 734)

Why is life? What is life? I'm not sure. I don't know if I'll ever be sure. You've been gone for two years now, Rob. The years are flying by. I've adjusted to your death, but the pain is still there. The fingers of that pain don't reach out into the rest of my life like they used to, but if I step into the room of memories, the pain still sears its way through me. I've adjusted to your death, but I'll never get used to it, nor will it ever be okay.

June 11th (Day 738)

It's been quite a week, Rob. I took a day off to spend some time at your grave and to deal with the pain that still exists around losing you. My friend, Alice, wanted to be with me. She seems to understand that just because two years have passed, that doesn't mean that the pain is gone. It's contained. I keep it in this room in my heart called "Rob," and the room is not opened to the general public very often. But, it's there . . . with all its contents—pain, joy, and memories.

The day started out quietly enough. Alice came over, and we went to your grave. We sat on the ground by your marker, talking, crying, sharing. As I was talking about you, I was gazing out across the lake, and out of the corner of my eye, I saw a red pickup driving quite fast on the road on the other side of the lake. As the pickup approached the trees across the lake, it disappeared from view, but I became aware of another vehicle behind the trees.

Suddenly we heard this smash and realized that the pickup had slammed into the back of the car. Then the car doors opened, and a voice shouted, "What the hell did you do that for?" In the next instant, we hear, "pop, pop, pop," and without any hesitation, both Alice and I knew we had just heard gunfire. We simultaneously looked at each other with semi-panicked faces, grabbed the blanket we had been sitting on and raced for her car. Her hands were shaking so badly she had to struggle to unlock the door.

Our minds were racing. To us it appeared as though the red pickup had deliberately smashed into the back of the car, then the driver of the pickup got out and shot the driver of the car. In our minds, we expected the pickup to come racing around the corner of the trees, realize we were witnesses, and shoot us. As we got into Alice's car, I grabbed her car phone to call 911, and she started backing out of the cemetery. We couldn't go straight ahead because that route would have taken us right by the two vehicles.

I couldn't get through to 911. I got a recording asking me to hold. Our hearts were beating so fast, they almost hurt. Once we got onto the main road and the pickup wasn't following us, we relaxed a tiny bit. I was still on "hold" with 911. We drove to Dad's office about three miles away, and I was still on "hold."

Chuck said when we walked into his office, we were both as white as sheets and shaking. I asked him to dial 911 and when they answered, they had already had a report of the shooting.

After we told Chuck what happened and we calmed down a bit, we realized that we needed to go back to witness as to what had happened. We didn't know if anyone else had been there or not.

Chuck went back to the cemetery with us, and it turned out that the shooting had been between the father and son of the family who owns the funeral home and cemetery. The father apparently had a drinking problem, and they had been quarreling about money for some time.

The father called that morning and told the son he was going to kill him. The final result was that the father was driving the pickup, he chased his son around the cemetery, slammed into the back of the son's car, and then got out of his pickup with a shotgun that he rested on the door of the vehicle and aimed. His son had to shoot back in self defense. The father died shortly after being rushed to the hospital.

It was really hard for me to understand. Here I was, grieving after two years without you, still feeling the pain and sense of loss that your absence has brought to my life, and a father deliberately set out to harm his son—over money! Life makes no sense.

The man who did the shooting was the man from whom we had purchased your grave plot. It was rather eerie that I happened to be there the day he killed his father.

What is life all about? Does anybody know? Does anybody have any answers? I keep beseeching God, but He's either not telling me or I'm not listening.

June 21st (Day 748)

Sing to me of dreams...
my dreams.
What dreams?
Dreams that long ago died
or never were.

Which?
I know not.
Dreaming seems
so foreign to me.
I don't know if
I ever experienced it.

Perhaps once . . .
before the pain . . .
before the death of my son.

But dream now,
my soul encourages.
Why?
I scream in return.

Why should I dream
only to have those dreams
trampled before my very eyes
as heavenly laughter echoes
through the skies.

I can't take that pain . . .
not again.
But what choice have I?
To never dream again?
To never try?

That's not much of a choice.
Not much of a life.

June 22nd (Day 749)

Trees move gently
to the rhythm
of the wind.

As my mind moves softly
to the beating
of my heart.

Keep your beating gentle
oh my heart,
so my mind won't race,

In a frantic, frenzied chase
for answers and reasons
that my gentle, beating heart
already knows.

August 12th (Day 800)

Life is perplexing, confusing, delightful and painful . . . rolled up like a snowball that has picked up the rocks and debris lying under the bright, white blanket of freshly fallen snow.

My life is like that. My present is the blanket of snow; my past, the rocks and debris that are hidden just below. It doesn't take much effort to get to the debris. As the white blanket of happiness, contentment, self-esteem grows thicker, the creations of my everyday existence are less convoluted by the junk under the surface.

Let it snow...let it snow!

September 27th (Day 846)

I made it through to my forty-fifth birthday, and my only regret is that you and Lori weren't here to celebrate it with me.

Dad had a surprise party for me, and it was Alice's job to get me away from the house without me being suspicious. (I had this little inkling that something was going on!)

Alice suggested we take a small picnic lunch and go to the cemetery to spend lunchtime with you. It was nice. I know I can talk to you anytime, but it was nice, for a change, to sit by your grave with a friend and laugh. I shared stories about you. Alice feels as though she knows you, even though I didn't meet her until about a year ago. She's never lost a child, yet is sensitive to things I need in connection with you. That helps me see that it can be done. You don't have to lose a child to be able to help someone through it. The difference is, Alice isn't afraid of emotions. She isn't afraid of me voicing them, nor is she afraid of being confronted with my feelings, my pain, my memories. That attitude, in itself, has helped me heal more than any other one thing.

I think you were with us today, and I believe you enjoyed the lunch and the time together as much as I did.

October 10th (Day 859)

Contentment falls softly
like a gentle snowfall.
You don't really know
it's there,
until the ground
is covered in white.

December 8th (Day 918)

You would have been twenty three years old today. Your birthday is still very hard for me. Today I thought about the day you were born. You were such a "wrinkled old man" when you first arrived in this life. Your face looked like it had the "wisdom of the ages" in it.

I was looking at your pictures last night and reflecting back and noticing the smile you almost always had on your face. You loved life! Even with the many ups and downs it had for you, you loved it! How did you do that? I could sure use you here to give me some pointers. I'm getting better, getting back to where I used to be—optimistic, happy—but I'm not quite there yet.

Your sister called me at work today. She knew it would be a hard day. She was having a tough one herself. You made a lasting impact on Lori, Dad, and me. That, in itself, could be a part of what life is all about—to make a difference, even if it's in just one person's life!

This morning I was having a hard time keeping the tears back at work, and I snapped at Shauna, our receptionist. I quickly apologized and explained to her that today would have been your birthday and that it was a tough day for me. After lunchtime, she walked into my office with a vase that had a red rose surrounded with greenery and baby's breath. I was so touched! Tears started flowing, Shauna put her arms around me, and I stood in the circle of her arms and sobbed. It was a warm, caring moment. When people just reach out and show they understand and care, it goes such a very long way.

Happy Birthday, my Rob.

December 15th (Day 925)

I could go on writing to you forever, Rob, and perhaps I will; but it's time to put this part to rest . . . time to see if it can help others. Time . . .

As the Bible says: "To every thing there is a season, and a time to every purpose under heaven: a time to be born, and a time to die; a time to weep, and a time to laugh; a time to mourn, and a time to dance."

It's time. Time for me to move forward and once again embrace every facet of life. Time for me to fully discover who I am now . . . because I have changed. I am not the same. But that's okay . . . change is not bad, I just have to get acquainted with the woman I am now.

I sense a wisdom and compassion that were not there before. I wonder what other traits I will discover that will be like diamonds that were formed under the blackness of my despair. It's time to now bring those gems to light and share them with the world.

I will never forget you. I will never "be okay" with the fact that you are now gone. And I will always love you and be thankful that you were a part of my life. I will still talk with you in the privacy of my mind and about you when the moments arise, but it is now time for me to once again fully engage with life.

I love you, my precious son, but it is now time.

Epilogue

It's been quite a few years since my son died, and life has gone on. I have cried and I have laughed; I have mourned and I have danced. Although the years keep passing, the story of my journey through grief is just as poignant as when I first wrote it. And other parents continue to lose children. Every time I watch the news and hear of the death of a child, I shudder at the journey of pain and suffering upon which those parents are embarking. It's a path with sharp turns of agony and rugged rocks of despair without any warning or comfort.

When I was in the midst of my grief, I wanted to read the words of other parents who had gone through the agony, because people who haven't, although they care and try to be kind, do not understand that you don't "move on" in a day, a month, or even a year. Grief, especially that associated with losing a child, takes its own course and its own time.

Although I had intended to publish this book within a year or two of my son's death, I was not ready. The pain revealed in this book is at times so raw that it has taken me some time to be able to release it into the world.

I remember that my grandmother, who had lost a son in the Korean War, would still talk about him forty years later. At the time, I couldn't understand it. I believed, as many people do, that her talking about him meant that she wasn't moving on or she hadn't healed. Now I know that is not true. Our children will continue to be a part of our lives forever . . . whether or not they leave this earth before us. And if there was any one piece of "advice" that I would give to parents who have lost children, it would be to not let others tell you how you should remember your children or the timeframe in which you should "move on," because only your own heart and soul have the right answer for you.

My son Rob will always live in my heart and soul, and I still have a picture of him in my office near the desk where I write. He—along with my daughter Lori and my grandchildren, Christopher, Hillary, and Tessa—are at the core of what I love and what my life is about.

Sadly, my marriage to Chuck didn't survive, but we both healed and found love again. Life goes on.

My dear grieving parent . . . losing a child is the hardest thing you will ever go through, but love yourself and be good to yourself through the process. You will survive and you will go on, and although you have paid the price with gut-wrenching pain, you will become stronger and wiser from the process.

I send loving and healing thoughts from my heart to yours.

Terri Ann Leidich

About The Author

Terri Ann Leidich is a freelance writer and author who lives in Christianburg, Virginia, with her husband Glenn. Although writing has been a part of Terri's business career for over thirty years, she has just begun to share her personal journeys and the style of writing that is her passion and life's purpose.

She recently released *For a Grieving Heart*.